Living with
DIVORCE AND FAMILY ISSUES

DR PARVATHY PATHY,
DR ANN-MARIE LO CASTRO, FOO CIRONG

Marshall Cavendish
Editions

Illustrations by Julie Davey
Series Designer: Bernard Go

First published 2003 by Times Editions

This 2015 edition published by
Marshall Cavendish Editions
An imprint of Marshall Cavendish International
1 New Industrial Road, Singapore 536196

Other Marshall Cavendish Offices
Marshall Cavendish Corporation. 99 White Plains Road, Tarrytown NY 10591-9001, USA • Marshall Cavendish International (Thailand) Co Ltd. 253 Asoke, 12th Flr, Sukhumvit 21 Road, Klongtoey Nua, Wattana, Bangkok 10110, Thailand • Marshall Cavendish (Malaysia) Sdn Bhd, Times Subang, Lot 46, Subang Hi-Tech Industrial Park, Batu Tiga, 40000 Shah Alam, Selangor Darul Ehsan, Malaysia

Marshall Cavendish is a trademark of Times Publishing Limited.

National Library Board, Singapore Cataloguing-in-Publication Data
Pathy, Parvathy, author.
Living with divorce and family issues / Dr Parvathy Pathy, Dr Ann-Marie Lo Castro, Foo Cirong ; illustrations by Julie Davey. – Second edition. – Singapore : Marshall Cavendish Editions, 2015.
pages cm – (Living with)
"First published 2003 by Times Editions."
ISBN : 978-981-4634-19-9 (paperback)

1. Children of divorced parents – Psychology. 2. Children of divorced parents – Family relationships. 3. Divorce – Psychological aspects. I. Title. II. Lo Castro, Ann-Marie, author. III. Foo, Cirong, author. IV. Davey, Julie, illustrator. V. Series: Living with.

HQ777.5
306.89 -- dc23   OCN914995293

Printed in Singapore by Markono Print Media Pte Ltd

Dedicated to
all the children of the
Child Guidance Clinic and their parents

CONTENTS

PREFACE

Divorce rates all over the world are rising in tandem with changing lifestyles and expectations that come with modernisation. However, divorce is still a traumatic event for all parties concerned – the couple that is no longer able to live together, their children, the in-laws, and the friends and acquaintances. All parties are invariably affected to some degree by news of a divorce. Often, it is the children who are the worst hit. Unlike adults who can turn to friends, counsellors or relatives for support and advice, children are often left in the lurch; they have no one to turn to for help and support, and no one seems to understand their distress.

This should not be the case. Adults, especially parents, have a responsibility to help their children cope with the impact of divorce. This is not an easy task, as the parent, especially the one who is being divorced, is also hurting and has to cope with caring for the children, new routines and lifestyle, and added responsibilities as a single parent. It is worse when the parent has to shoulder the financial burden alone and also has to go out to work at the same time. Nevertheless, it is still possible for parents facing a marital and family break-up to help their children cope with their divorce.

This book aims to help divorced parents understand how divorce affects children and how they can help their children cope with the potential negative impacts of divorce. Other adults, such as aunts, uncles or grandparents, can also use this book to help children under their care who are hurting from their parents' divorce. This book serves to answer common questions and issues that arise as divorced parents learn to reorganise their lives and move on to a new life phase, either alone or with a new family or partner.

Dr Parvathy Pathy
July 2015

INTRODUCTION

Divorce in any family constitutes a big transition and major adjustment for children. Children may experience and display several emotional and behavioural reactions to the divorce and the 'loss' of one parent. This book hopes to help parents understand the psychosocial and emotional impacts of their divorce on their children so that they can help to minimise their children's pain and distress over the family break-up.

The way children react to their parents' divorce is strongly influenced by the way in which their parents behave before, during and after the separation or divorce. Children will need greater support, sensitivity and love to help them overcome the loss that they experience during this difficult time. Like their parents who experience grief from the divorce, children have similar feelings of sadness, anger, denial, fear and guilt. Such children may develop adjustment difficulties in the form of emotional and behavioural problems, difficulties with studies or social withdrawal.

Children whose parents are divorced often feel different from their peers. They have burning questions about what has happened and about their future:

- Why can't my parents stay together anymore?
- When will the divorce be over?
- Will they still be my parents?
- What is going to happen to me?
- Will my parents abandon me, like they have left the marriage ?

This book attempts to create a greater awareness and understanding of the world of children whose parents have divorced or are in the midst of it. Some specific case studies are used to illustrate the difficulties that parents commonly experience and effective ways to deal with them.

This book also highlights issues related to the spectrum of emotional distancing or emotional absence in intact families or families going through the process of divorce.

It is our hope that this book will help parents, who are undergoing the process of divorce, minimise its impact on their children who are also going through a difficult, bewildering and painful period.

WHAT DOES DIVORCE MEAN TO A CHILD?

PART 1

There are some children who never outgrow the impact of their parents' divorce. Feelings of hurt, anger, abandonment and of being unloved may continue to linger in their hearts even after they become adults. Therefore, it is important for parents to continue to care for and love their children even after their marriage is over.

A child may often experience several common emotions during and after his parents' separation or divorce. To help the child cope with the loss, it is crucial that his parents help him acknowledge and resolve these different feelings.

1.1   HOW MAY CHILDREN REACT NEGATIVELY TO A DIVORCE?

Some children may suffer detrimental effects to their self-esteem to the extent that they view themselves as 'bad' children who have caused their parents to divorce. This is especially the case with younger children who tend to be egocentric and think that the world revolves around them.

From a child's perspective, the events that occur around him are caused by his behaviour, thoughts and wishes. Thus, the child may blame himself for his parents' divorce and conclude that he does not deserve the good things in life. The child may even perceive himself as being unfortunate and deprived, in having to adjust to the various changes in his family and in his life.

Some children idolise their parents. When things go wrong between his parents, the child may not be able to accept that his 'perfect' parents are at fault. He will find it easier to blame himself than think negatively of his parents. Thus, the child gets saddled with needless guilt and develops a negative self-image.

Through an unconscious mechanism, children may also overachieve to get their parents' attention and save their marriage. Children may also have an urgent need to feel loved and accepted by others. Such unrealistic demands and expectations may continue into adulthood and have a negative impact on the child's future relationships.

1.2   WHAT ARE SOME COMMON REACTIONS TO DIVORCE?

Denial

Denial is one method a child may use to cope with his emotional pain and protect himself from feelings of betrayal, anger and sadness. When a child hears about his parents' divorce, his first reaction may be disbelief, especially if the news had come without warning. A child in denial may choose to ignore the news or cling to the belief that his parents' separation and problems are only temporary. He may refuse to talk about the situation and instead make up wonderful stories about his family.

The child's prolonged denial of his parents' or family situation may be an indication of self-blame. If a child believes that he is the reason for his parents' divorce, he may become overly obliging in the hope that his parents will reunite. The child may harbour reunification fantasies about his parents. He may even try to play peacemaker to help them reconcile.

It is important to note that while denial may help to shield a child against his initial shock, persistent denial will compromise his ability to cope with the divorce and move on in his life. It will also affect the child's ability to successfully negotiate and overcome the various developmental stages and different challenges in his life.

Sadness, hurt and loss

Sadness is the most pervasive reaction in children when their parents break up. A child will get very upset when his parents do not get along well, especially if they are constantly physically or verbally abusing each other. A child will usually feel sad about his parents' break-up, even if there had been constant fights and arguments at home.

For a child, a parent's place in his life is usually irreplaceable. When one parent leaves, the child may think that the parent no longer cares about him. This leaves him feeling rejected and unloved. The child's sadness about the family break-up may be expressed through crying or a glum and sad demeanour. The child may become reserved and lethargic or daydream often.

Some parents think that leaving the marital home in a secret but sudden manner will shield the child from the negative impact of the separation and stop the child from asking them difficult and awkward questions. However, the parent's sudden departure from the family, without adequate preparation or a proper farewell, only serves to heighten the child's feelings of loss, insecurity and unpredictability in his life. Such feelings are detrimental to the child's sense of security, emotional well-being and development.

The emotional hurt that a child feels is usually amplified when the parent who leaves the home does not keep in regular contact with him. In cases where a child is abandoned by a parent, he may feel rejected, unworthy and suffer from a low self-esteem.

Worry

Children may suffer from worry as a result of the helplessness and insecurity brought on by their parents' break-up. The child's worries and fears are accentuated if the remaining parent is distressed, depressed or suicidal and appears incapable of looking after the children or handling the home situation. Issues that may worry the children include :

- What will happen after one parent leaves the home?
- Will their various needs still be met?
- Will the remaining parent also abandon them?
- Will they have to move home and change school?
- Will they still get to see the parent who has left?

The child may demonstrate this worry by excessive crying or clinging to a parent, or having a need to hang on to a beloved object that he had already outgrown, such as a stuffed toy. He may have nightmares, poor sleep, poor appetite or lose interest in playing or studying.

Anger

Children who feel abandoned and unloved may experience intense feelings of anger. Such children may get angry for a variety of reasons. However, due to their young age and immaturity, these children will not be able to understand or label the various emotions that they may be feeling. Even several years after their parent's divorce, some of these angry children remain upset and angry about the family break-up. This anger may be directed at one or both parents and lead to problems for themselves.

Children may even blame the parent who had filed for divorce or walked out on the family. A child may blame his parents for causing him misery because of the many difficult changes that came with the divorce. He may angrily view his parents as being selfish or incapable of protecting him from his pain. He may even start wondering why his parents got married in the first place. The child's anger may be expressed as irritation towards his parents or quarrelsome, aggressive and disobedient behaviour towards other adults or children in his life. The child may reject the parent with whom he is angry with, and refuse to have any contact or interaction with that parent. Sometimes, the child may even lash out in anger at the parent he is living with.

In school, a child's anger may be expressed through aggressive acts such as throwing objects, stealing, vandalism or fighting with peers. Some children act up by refusing to do their homework. Some of the child's actions end up being so disruptive that he ends up facing disciplinary action at school. These behavioural problems are just some manifestations of how angry and unhappy the child is feeling about his parents' divorce.

These problems indicate that the child is unable to accept and resolve his feelings about his parents' divorce and the new family situation. His parents need to help him express his anger in a more appropriate and safe manner. Even though the child's parents should understand that their child's aggressive and difficult behaviour is the result of his emotional disturbance, they should still set limits on their child's destructive behaviour. In addition, the parents should help the child talk about his various feelings about the divorce. Children need time to resolve their anger. It is essential for parents to demonstrate their continuous support and care at this time, even though the family break-up is equally difficult for them.

Guilt

A child normally allocates a reason to an event. He may naively believe that his parents are divorcing because of him, especially when his parents do not speak to him and explain the reason for their break-up. Young children, for instance, may believe that their actions, such as being disobedient, not completing homework or talking back to a parent, may have driven away their parent. Even though older children may know that the divorce is not their fault, they may still feel guilty for not being 'better' children.

In very chaotic families, where parents are constantly quarrelling or fighting, a child may sometimes feel that it would be better if his parents did not stay together. When the parents eventually separate and divorce, the fighting and constant turmoil in the home ends and the child finally experiences some measure of peace and relief. However, the child may still feel conflicted and guilty for harbouring such ambivalent feelings and wishes about his parents. He may still hope that his parents could be happily together.

1.3   WHAT ARE SOME CHANGES CHILDREN FACE AFTER A DIVORCE?

For most families, divorce means re-adapting to life and having to make several significant changes. The children usually have to face practical changes that may require major adjustments, such as switching to a new school, moving to a new and smaller house, assuming more household responsibilities, adjusting to new childcare arrangements and perhaps staying with step-parents. The lifestyle changes may be gradual or they may occur at a time when the children are emotionally grappling with various feelings associated with the loss of a parent or their former lifestyle. These important changes add to the stress that the family is already feeling, and may disrupt the routine that the children have been accustomed to. Children with poor coping skills and low adaptive abilities are most likely to feel overwhelmed and stressed by the onslaught of so many accompanying changes.

A new home
Children may have to move to a new home after their parents' divorce. Usually, the new home is less ideal compared to the familiar home they are used to. Some families may purchase smaller flats to stay in, while others are forced to stay with relatives or friends until they can afford to move out. These changes can be hard on children, especially if they live with friends or relatives and have to cope with new house rules and routines.

Infants may experience disruptions in their sleep and eating patterns, and preschoolers may cry excessively or become clingy and fussy. Older children may resent not having enough privacy and having to depend on someone else's family.

A new school
Some children may have to be enrolled in a new school if their current school is too far away from their new home. This means that they may face some difficulty in maintaining the friendships they had formed in the current school.

Attending a new school also means that the child has to adjust to a different environment. He has to get used to new teachers and teaching styles, adapt to new rules and find new friends. All these can be quite threatening as the child tries to find a niche for himself. All these changes can add on to the stress that the child is already facing from his parents' divorce. For children who are not sociable or outgoing, making new friends is often a difficult and formidable task. The resultant social anxiety may aggravate their emotional distress and insecurity, causing them to dread school. Younger children may become clingier and revert to regressive behaviour, such as soiling themselves or bed-wetting.

More/new responsibilities

Some children have to cope with housework and taking care of younger siblings, if the custodial parent has to work to support the family.

Older children, in particular, may be tasked with household chores such as doing the laundry, cleaning the house and preparing the meals. They may also have to ensure that their younger siblings complete their homework, take their meals and wash up. Some children also take it upon themselves to either physically or emotionally care for their parent, who may be emotionally devastated by the divorce. Some of these children do not allow themselves to grieve, as they have to focus all their energies on their emotionally distraught parent. This robs them the chance to mix with their or peers and engage in age-appropriate leisure or academic pursuits.

New caregiver

When custodial parents have to work to support the family, they have to make new childcare arrangements for young children. This may include getting relatives to look after the children, hiring a nanny, putting the child in a childcare centre or student care centre.

Unfortunately, most young children initially experience significant difficulty in adapting to the change in routine. Besides having to adjust to a new environment and a new caregiver, children have to deal with having less time and attention from their parents. A child, especially a young child, may experience significant emotional disturbance when he is being separated from his custodial parent. The child may worry that his remaining parent may abandon him and display his anxiety through excessive crying, temper tantrums, clinginess or regressive behaviour.

1.4   TO WHAT EXTENT ARE CHILDREN AFFECTED BY THEIR PARENTS' DIVORCE?

The impacts of divorce on a child depend on several factors, namely:

- his age and personality or temperamental traits,
- the type of relationship he has with his parents and other supportive adults,
- the manner in which the divorce is explained to him,
- the number and type of lifestyle changes he has to make after the family break-up,

- the way his parents relate with one another and communicate regarding child custody or access issues.

1.5 WHAT IS EMOTIONAL ABSENCE AND ITS EFFECT ON CHILDREN?

A child whose parent is physically present, but disengaged, distracted or emotionally distant, may display similar emotional or behavioural difficulties and issues as the child whose parents are divorced.

A child who feels ignored or unloved by his parents may have feelings of rejection, poor self-worth and sadness as the child's need for closeness, emotional warmth and attachment remains unmet. A child whose emotional needs are unmet may become needy, fretful, irritable or angry. A parent who is emotionally absent may cause a child to feel confused. A child may not understand why he is being ignored. He will feel worthless, depressed or become withdrawn.

'Ghost parents' refers to parents who are emotionally neglectful or who are uninvolved in their children's day-to-day life. These parents are often absorbed in their own world or may be feeling rejected as a result of their failed marriage. Consequently, they are unable to focus on their child's emotional needs.

There is often no emotional engagement with the child and the child is left to resolve his own emotional needs and issues. The child may then experience frustration, anger, loneliness and a longing for emotional attachment and attention from his parent.

Depending on their age, emotional development and cognitive abilities, the child may feel bad or unlovable. Meanwhile, the parent who is emotionally absent remains unaware of the events happening in his child's life and the child's feelings and needs. In order to compensate, the child may unconsciously attempt to attract attention and win his parents' love by externalising his sense of self-worth (e.g. placing too much emphasis on achievements and gift-giving rather than building his inner self-esteem) or engage in difficult, regressive or negative behaviours. The child may steal to 'comfort' himself or to unconsciously get his parents' attention. He may neglect his homework or start to fight with his classmates.

When a parent is emotionally absent, the child may become parentified and assume duties and responsibilities beyond his years in order to make up for the feelings of abandonment he is experiencing. The parentified child or adolescent may be expected to take care of younger siblings by helping with the feeding, bathing and housework. Furthermore, the parentified child may need to be a source of emotional support to the remaining parent, as the parent may be too upset to care for himself or herself. This parentification of the child and the associated inappropriate role-reversal may be detrimental to the child's emotional well-being and development.

For a child, having an absent parent may also lead to a lack of opportunities to socialise with peers and participate in usual activities that help to develop his sense of self-competence and self-identity. A healthy and secure attachment during the child's early years helps the child to:

- develop intellectually,
- attain perceptual awareness,
- develop resilience and coping abilities to manage stress and fear appropriately,
- develop healthy peer and adult relationships,
- attain appropriate levels of self-confidence, self-worth and contentment.

Every child is different. Different children react in different ways to the same challenges in their life. However, it is still helpful for parents to understand the typical feelings and behaviour that are prominent across different age groups. It is also essential for parents to try to maintain the child's routine and to adequately prepare the child for any changes, so as to reduce further stress for the child.

Age-specific reactions to parental divorce or separation
Infants and toddlers may:
- show irritable behaviour such as crying and being fussy,
- show changes in sleep patterns and other daily routines,
- feel fear and anxiety towards new adults in the family,
- have difficulty in being away from parents,
- have nightmares,
- display anger, often as tantrums,
- become clingy towards caregivers.

Preschoolers may:
- worry about their safety or whether they are loved,
- become clingy and refuse to be separated from their caregivers,

- deny that the divorce is real,
- believe that they are the cause of the divorce,
- be overly obliging,
- show regressive behaviour, such as thumb-sucking, bed-wetting and being overly clingy,
- hit peers or younger siblings,
- have nightmares.

Children in primary school may:
- feel different from their peers and stigmatised,
- blame every disappointment on the divorce,
- assume blame, so as to feel more in control,
- withdraw from company or become aggressive,
- harbour fantasies about their parents reuniting,
- be sensitive and more attuned to how their parents are feeling,
- be overly obliging,
- do poorly in school,
- lack concentration,
- take sides with either parent, rejecting one parent in the process.

Pre-teens and adolescents may:
- have difficulty accepting the reality of changes caused by the divorce,
- feel abandoned by the parent who leaves,
- feel angry with the parent who initiated the divorce, even if there had been marital violence or infidelity by the other parent,
- withdraw from long-time friends and favourite activities,
- become more aggressive and rebellious towards teachers and parents,
- lose interest in studies,
- engage in unacceptable activities, such as stealing and truancy,
- feel angry and unsure of their beliefs about love, marriage and family,
- experience a sense of having grown up too soon,
- worry about 'adult matters' such as the family's financial security,
- feel obligated to take on more adult responsibilities in the family,
- feel different from their peers and stigmatised.

HELPING CHILDREN
COPE WITH DIVORCE

PART 2

Many parents continue to fight behind or in front of their children even after they have divorced. This only serves to hurt the children as it puts them in the midst of their parents' unresolved conflicts. Often, the children hear bad things about one parent from the other or witness ugly parental quarrels and fights. Children may feel pressured to take sides or to mediate and defuse the tension between their parents. This is probably a lot more than they can handle emotionally.

2.1 MY HUSBAND SAYS HE WANTS A DIVORCE. DESPITE MY PLEAS FOR RECONCILIATION, HE IS ADAMANT ABOUT HIS DECISION. WHAT AM I SUPPOSED TO DO WITH MY THREE YOUNG CHILDREN?

It must be devastating to hear that your partner wants a divorce. It would be helpful to first get support for yourself, especially emotional support, from a close friend, relative or professional counsellor. As you become emotionally stronger, you can help your children cope better. At this stage, there are several things you can do for your children.

Explain to the children that you and your husband are getting a divorce. You can tell them that the two of you are no longer going to be married to each other and will be living apart. However, reassure them that you are both still their parents and will continue to love them.

Let them know how the divorce is going to affect them. For example, you can tell them that they will stay with you in the same house while their father moves out, or that they will move with you to another house and may have to attend another school.

Reassure them that you will continue to take care of them. Your children will probably be worried that you may abandon them. Enlist the help of other adults if you are too distressed to support or care for your children on your own.

Despite the anger and hurt that you may feel towards your husband, it is important for you to encourage your children to maintain a good relationship with him. Although this is often a very difficult task, especially in the early stages when the emotional wounds are raw and deep, your children will benefit from having a good relationship with both parents.

Try to identify other adults who can give your children additional support. This will minimise the burden on you as your children can bring their troubles to someone who is emotionally detached from the situation. A child may feel more at ease discussing certain issues with an outsider, as he may not want to burden an already distressed parent.

Help your children develop their self-esteem and sense of security. These are two important aspects which suffer when parents divorce. Children may feel ashamed, embarrassed and devalued as a result of the divorce.

Reassure the children that the divorce is not their fault. Sometimes children think that their misbehaviours may have caused their parents' divorce. This needless guilt is a heavy burden for a child to carry and can lead to persistent emotional or behavioural problems.

Try to maintain a cordial relationship with your ex-husband. Research and clinical experience have shown that children adjust better and faster to a divorce when their parents co-operate and co-parent harmoniously. If issues are not resolved adequately or in an acrimonious manner, the children may be adversely affected and scarred.

2.2   WHAT CAN I DO TO HELP MY CHILDREN DEAL WITH THE IMPACT OF MY DIVORCE?

Children at different ages are at different stages of development. By recognising these stages, you can help them better adjust to the divorce.

Infants and toddlers

Infants and toddlers are starting to build trust and form attachments. They are terrified of separation and can be very difficult to manage during the transition periods when they return to one parent after a visit with the other. It is therefore essential to minimise changes in the home and establish as much consistency and familiarity as possible. One way is to have the same person tuck them into bed every night. Sometimes it is better for an infant or toddler to have only short daytime access with the non-custodial parent. Overnight access should be granted only when the child is ready to separate from the custodial parent without significant and persistent distress.

Children in this age group do not have a good notion of the passage of time. Therefore, the period of separation from the main caregiver parent may seem endless. The children's limited vocabulary at this stage makes it difficult for them to express their fears and insecurities to adults. These children are more likely to express their discomfort, fear or frustration by throwing tantrums or crying.

It is essential that these children are given plenty of assurance through verbal and physical affection. Singing to them or hugging them will help to soothe them. You can also help ease their anxiety by spending more time with them while getting them ready for visits with the other parent. You can also let them bring their favourite toy, or a familiar item to comfort them while they are away from home and in their non-custodial parent's home. During the access with the non-custodial parent, it will be helpful if the child is allowed to keep in touch with the custodial parent via short telephone conversations.

It is important keep to normal schedules especially with regard to feeding and sleeping times. Talk to your ex-spouse about ways to maintain consistency in the time he or she spends with the child. Ideally, the child should not be unnecessarily separated from his usual caregiver. The non-custodial parent should be allowed regular access (unless there are significant safety concerns) so as to maintain a good parent-child relationship. Access can be gradually increased when the child feels more comfortable being away from his main caregiver.

Preschoolers

Children at this stage are often confused about the cause of their parents' divorce. Preschoolers and older children generally ponder on this and are likely to blame themselves for 'chasing away' the other parent. They may change to become extremely obedient and do nice things to please their parents in the hope of bringing them back together. They may have ideas such as "If I'm really good, Mummy and Daddy will get back together again." It is important for parents to assure their child that the divorce is not of his doing. They should also gently address the impossibility of getting back together. The child should be discouraged from believing that his parents will one day reunite.

Some children may become aggressive and violent as a result of their emotional disturbance regarding their parents' divorce. Although parents should try to empathise with their child's emotional distress, they still need to take immediate action to set limits on such negative behaviour and enforce appropriate disciplinary measures, as they would do in a normal family situation. It is helpful for the child to express his anger in a more appropriate manner. Parents who discipline their children for aggressive behaviour are, in fact, helping them feel safe and secure by containing their overwhelming emotions. Parents could explore healthier ways for their children to express their anger, such as talking to an adult or through art. Reading suitable children's books on managing one's emotions or dealing with parental divorce can also help young children understand and manage their feelings of anger, sadness and fear in more appropriate ways.

The stress of divorce may also cause preschoolers to respond by displaying regressive behaviours such as bed-wetting, temper tantrums and clinginess. Although these behaviours can be frustrating, parents should be aware that these are the mechanisms that young children unconsciously use to help them deal with the trauma of losing a parent. Basically, regressive behaviour helps the child retreat mentally until he is better able to grapple with his emotions. It is normal for such behaviour to go on for a few months. Parents need to provide plenty of assurance and love to their children at this stage of their adjustment.

Children in primary school

Primary school children usually have a better but limited understanding of life and are beginning to empathise with others. They may start worrying about being deprived of food, toys or attention. They may wonder about their parents' ability to look after them after the divorce. It is important for parents to reassure their children that despite their divorce, they will still love them and provide care and protection.

Some children may be preoccupied with feelings of rejection, loss, guilt and conflict of loyalty. As a result, they may have poor concentration and do badly in school. They may become easily irritable and get into fights with other children or they may choose to withdraw from their peers.

It is important that parents avoid:
• putting their child in a position where he is forced to take sides,
• arguing in front of the child,
• speaking ill of their ex-spouse no matter how hurt they are, as this often backfires and leads to the child disliking both parents.

For the well-being of the child, it is important to encourage him to love the other parent. Children can read their parents' moods and may be emotionally affected if they see their parents displaying negative behaviour. Parents who set aside special time to be with their children are likely to create an environment where the children can feel safe. In such a safe environment, children may be more willing to talk to their parents about the issues that trouble or perplex them.

CASE STUDY

SHAH, THE GO-BETWEEN

Six-year-old Shah often threw temper tantrums during the period her parents were separated. Her father used her as a messenger to persuade her mother not to divorce him. Shah became trapped in her parents' marital problems. She felt that she was to blame for not being able to get her parents back together.

Shah's mother had a talk with her about her feelings towards the separation. An empathetic listener, she helped Shah identify her sense of loss, helplessness and anger. She reassured Shah that her parents would always be there for her, and would care for and love her as before. She also spoke to her husband, calmly reiterating that the marriage was over and that nothing could bring them back together again. He eventually came to accept the irreversibility of the marital breakdown and stopped using Shah to carry messages. Over time, Shah stopped throwing tantrums.

Pre-teens and adolescents

Children in this age group generally tend to be self-conscious, idealistic and rebellious. These children are in the process of forming their identities and making important life choices. When adolescents see their parents getting a divorce, they begin to question the notion of commitment and may become wary of getting hurt in relationships. These negative experiences may leave them feeling rejected and abandoned, and cause them to develop an unhealthy phobia about marriage and relationships. They may react to such negative feelings by turning to their peers for support.

It would be important for parents to ensure that their teenagers have adequate opportunities to talk about the divorce. Teenagers who are unable to do so may engage in unhelpful ways to cope with their difficult feelings, including drug and alcohol abuse, truancy, joining gangs, smoking, running away from home or engaging in offending behaviours. While trying to show empathy, parents still need to continue to set limits and implement consequences if their teenager misbehaves.

It is a good idea for parents to hold regular family meetings and engage in one-to-one conversations with their teenager. However, not all teenagers find it easy to talk to their parents about their personal feelings, especially if family members do not usually talk about feelings with one another. For teenagers who cannot communicate well, putting down their thoughts into words is a better way to express their feelings. Sometimes, external parties like a favourite aunt or school counsellor can be a valuable source of support for the teenager. Whichever is the chosen way, allow teenagers to find an outlet to express themselves appropriately so that they do not internalise or externalise all their frustrations and become depressed or destructive.

Parents who are emotionally overwhelmed may use their children as an emotional crutch and pour out their woes to them. One result is that some teenagers may take on the role of 'rescuer' to support the parent who is struggling to cope. As a result, these children are forced to behave in a more mature way than they actually are, when they should be engaged in more appropriate pursuits like making friends or focusing on their studies. Parents should avoid using their children as their emotional crutch.

Parents who are emotionally or psychologically distressed need to turn to other adults, such as friends and counsellors, for support and help. Parents should encourage their teenagers to spend more time on school and social activities that will provide them with more pleasant and rewarding experiences. It is important for parents to find out how their children are doing in school academically and socially when the family is going through an emotionally trying period. Sometimes this may involve sharing the family situation with a trusted teacher.

Finally, some teenage children may start worrying about financial issues especially if the parent expresses financial concerns frequently. Such teenagers will be distracted from studying and divert their time and energy towards working and earning money. This can lead to poor academic grades and premature termination of the teenager's educational pursuit. As far as possible, parents should shield their children from the family's financial situation. If necessary, parents can explain their financial situation to their children briefly and help them to live within the family's means. However, a teenager should not be expected to bear the brunt of providing for the family's financial needs at the expense of his educational progress.

2.2   SINCE THE EFFECTS OF DIVORCE ARE POTENTIALLY HARMFUL TO CHILDREN, SHOULD THEY BE SENT FOR THERAPY?

Not all children of divorced parents require therapy. However, most children are likely to develop some sort of acute reaction to their parents' separation. Temper tantrums, crying spells, withdrawal and disruptive behaviour are common.

Parents need to be sensitive to their children's possible emotional struggles. They must understand that children also go through the same emotional struggle that they, the adults, faced when confronted with the reality of their divorce.

Children need time to accept the situation and grieve for the leaving parent and the permanent loss of a normal family life. As children get used to the reality of living with only one parent, such reactions gradually disappear with support from their parents.

In general, children who exhibit persistently difficult behaviour that affects their well-being and functioning will need therapy. For children with pre-existing difficult behaviour or emotional difficulty, such difficulties can be aggravated by their parents' divorce. Should a child exhibit severely disturbed behaviours, he may require immediate attention. A good indicator of whether children are adversely affected by their parents' divorce is feedback from school teachers. Teachers spend a lot of time with children, so they may be more objective than parents in observing changes in the children's behaviour. Thus, it is important that parents communicate with their children's teachers both during and after the divorce period.

Tips to help children adjust to a divorce

- Affirm to your children that they are not responsible for your divorce
- Give them permission to love the non-custodial parent
- Try to maintain constant and cordial contact with your ex-spouse
- When speaking to your children about your ex-spouse, talk positively about him and avoid badmouthing him or her
- Help your children express their feelings through discussion, play or art
- Empathise with them and let them know you understand their feelings
- Establish and maintain daily routines, minimising changes as much as possible
- Set limits on undesirable or negative behaviour if needed
- Seek emotional support for yourself from appropriate sources

BEHAVIOURAL ISSUES
AFTER DIVORCE

Divorce does not only concern the two adults involved in the marriage. Children of the marriage are also adversely affected to a large extent.

When children are distressed, they may have difficulty expressing their feelings. The child may have feelings that are too intense and difficult for him to manage. Some children may try to hide their emotions so as not to make their parent worry about them. The emotional disturbance experienced by children may often be manifested through behavioural changes, both at home and in school. One common sign is a sudden fall in their school grades.

3.1   I FOUND MY YOUNG SON HOLDING ON TO HIS FATHER'S PHOTOGRAPH AND WHIMPERING. I WAS QUITE SHOCKED AS HE IS USUALLY TOUGH IN CHARACTER. I AM ALSO AS SAD AS HE IS. SHOULD I IGNORE THE SITUATION AND LET HIM BE?

Many parents, especially Asian parents, are reserved when it comes to the expression of emotions. They may think that displaying sadness is a sign of weakness. Parents often feel discomfort when they see their children crying, especially if these are boys. Children need to know that grieving and crying is a natural part of adjusting to their parents' divorce situation, and that they can share their feelings freely with their parents. When a sad child is comforted, he can then focus his energy on other meaningful and enjoyable activities that is appropriate for his age.

Avoid ignoring the situation in the belief that your son's sadness will fade away. He will have an easier time coming to terms with your divorce if you can help him to process his emotions and allow him to talk about his feelings. Refrain from criticising him or ignoring his sadness by saying things like, "Why are you crying for your father? He does not want us any more."

Boys, in particular, need more encouragement and support to express their grief. It is appropriate for parents to share some of their feelings about the divorce with their children, so that they know that they are not alone and that it is normal to feel sad. However, do not pour out all your heartache to your child and overwhelm him with all your negative emotions. If you need to unburden your emotional load and express your difficulties and distress, speak to a friend or counsellor instead.

3.2   I RECEIVED COMPLAINTS FROM MY 8-YEAR OLD SON'S TEACHER THAT HE HAS BEEN KICKING HIS CLASSMATES AND THROWING CHAIRS AROUND. BUT AT HOME, HE IS SWEET AND BEHAVES 'NORMALLY' EVEN AFTER MY DIVORCE. WHY IS THIS SO? HOW CAN I INTERVENE?

When a young child feels angry about his parents' divorce, he may not necessarily vent his anger at his parent. This is because he may fear that any nasty behaviour on his part will drive away the remaining parent.

Often, the pent-up anger is displaced on someone else. Parents experiencing such problems with their children should talk to them and try to understand why they are throwing tantrums and misbehaving in school.

Assist your son to talk about his anger instead of acting it out. You can also suggest other ways that will help him deal with his anger, such as:

- counting slowly from one to ten,
- breathing deeply until calm sets in,
- writing down the situations and thoughts that make him angry.

Together with your son, you may want to meet up with his teacher to discuss ways to set limits on his aggressive behaviour. One method the teacher can employ is to implement time-out. Not only will this help him learn to cool down, it will also prevent him from hurting others.

Check that your son is not blaming himself for the divorce. Your son may be having other underlying emotions that he is afraid to express at home for fear of upsetting you. A child who tries eagerly to convince his parents that he is alright may be denying his own feelings about the divorce. Talk to your son directly about how he feels about the divorce. If parents make an effort to talk to their children, they will be more willing to open up. However, if your son does not open up to you, you can get a counsellor or a trusted adult to talk to your child.

3.3   MY 4-YEAR-OLD DAUGHTER HAS BEEN THROWING TANTRUMS AND CRYING FREQUENTLY AFTER I SEPARATED FROM MY HUSBAND A FEW WEEKS AGO. IT ALWAYS TAKES MORE THAN AN HOUR TO PACIFY HER. WHAT SHOULD I DO?

Your child is probably missing her father and feeling sad and distressed by his absence. Not being able to understand that her parents' marriage has ended, she may be wondering where her father has gone and fear that you, too, will disappear. Children of this age may harbour fears that when a person is gone, that person may not return. This will make them feel anxious and afraid and cause them to throw tantrums.

There are a few strategies you can employ to help your child overcome her anxiety while she is waiting for the visits with her father. You could ask your daughter to circle on a calendar the dates of her father's visits. This way, your child can view her schedule with her father in a more concrete way.

You may wish to use time-out to control your daughter's tantrums. Take her to a quiet place away from the area of conflict, away from people and other distractions. Let her remain there until she has calmed down.

You may also discuss with your ex-spouse about having a more regular visiting schedule. Children of a young age benefit from more physical contact with each parent, especially if they are quite attached to the missing parent. If your child's behaviour remains unmanageable, allow daily telephone calls from her father. This will help to ease her separation anxiety until she becomes accustomed to his absence.

Try to understand her feelings and be extra supportive. If your daughter is able to verbalise her thoughts, chat with her to understand her fears and distress. However, if your daughter misbehaves, you should still discipline her and set reasonable limits. For example, you can withhold her toys if she does not stop whining. Make sure that the rules you set for your daughter are reasonable, clear and simple enough for her to understand. Give her lots of reinforcement, such as hugs and praise, when she stops whining and throwing a tantrum. Reassure her that you will be there for her even though her father is not around.

3.4   SINCE WE ANNOUNCED OUR DIVORCE, OUR TEENAGE SON HAS BECOME WITHDRAWN AND SHUTS HIMSELF IN HIS ROOM. HE HAS STOPPED GOING FOR HOCKEY TRAINING, WHICH WAS HIS PASSION. WE AVOIDED TALKING TO HIM ABOUT THE DIVORCE FOR FEAR THAT IT WOULD HURT HIM BUT NOW WE ARE CONCERNED ABOUT HIM. WHAT CAN WE DO TO GET HIM TO OPEN UP?

The more evasive parents are about their divorce, the more the child will feel rejected, as he may come to think that his feelings are of no importance. Your son may be experiencing a sense of loss and anger about what he is going through. If you refuse to talk to your son about the issue for fear of upsetting him, you may be subconsciously causing him to internalise self-blame and bottle up his feelings.

Be direct and honest with him about the divorce. Teenagers usually want to be treated like young adults. If you do this, your son will be able to cope with the divorce with more maturity. Although teenagers are more mature than younger children, they still need their parents' assurance and love. Let your son know that any money problems will be taken care of and assure him that he had nothing to do with the divorce. Reassure him that both of you will be there for him even after the divorce. As parents, keep to your word and maintain a good relationship with each other even after the divorce.

Finally, encourage your son to stay socially active. Find time to check up on how he feels and allow him to talk freely about his emotions.

3.5   I'M HAVING A HARD TIME WITH MY 5-YEAR-OLD SON AFTER SEPARATING FROM MY HUSBAND. IT IS IMPOSSIBLE FOR ME TO LEAVE THE HOUSE WITHOUT HIM CLINGING TO ME. HE CRIES FREQUENTLY AND IS ALWAYS CALLING ME AT WORK. WHAT CAN I DO TO STOP THIS BEHAVIOUR?

It seems that your son is worried about being abandoned. When one parent leaves the marital home, the child may fear that the remaining parent may also leave him. This heightens the child's fear and anxiety and causes him to exhibit clingy behaviour. You should try to talk to your son about his fears and help him to express them in a more acceptable way. You must stay calm and reassure him that you are not going to abandon him.

To avoid unnecessary disruptions at work, you should set aside a specific time to call home. Promise your child that you will talk to him at the same time every day and keep the promise. This can help alleviate his anxiety. Do not sneak out of the house without telling him where you are going. It will only aggravate your child's feelings of insecurity and make him more anxious and clingy.

If possible, bring your child to where you work so that he has a mental picture of where you are and what you do when you are away from home. When you are at work, assign him some tasks so that he focuses on something positive. For example, you could get him to colour a picture, complete a jigsaw puzzle or water the plants. If he completes these tasks, be sure to reward him when you get home. Assure your child that he will be safe with the caregiver. If you praise and reward him when he calls you less or cries less, he will learn that he can get your attention through positive behaviour.

CASE STUDY

LIVING IN THE SHADOW OF DIVORCE

"Look at how thin she is. Don't you feed her properly? What kind of a mother are you!" Mr Tan exclaimed to his ex-wife when he arrived to take his daughter out during a scheduled visit.

"How dare you say that? Who is responsible for her condition? You did not pay the maintenance amount on time last month. And you are late again this month!"

Serene stood quietly listening to the argument between her parents. This was a common scene played out by her parents every time her father visited her. She felt miserable and did not understand why her parents were always fighting over her. Deep inside her, she was crying for her parents to stop fighting. She felt lonely and scared. "Nobody really cares about me," she thought. "My parents would be happier if I am gone."

Serene lived in the shadow of her parents' contentious post-divorce relationship. She felt worthless and thought that life was meaningless.

Over time, her father drifted out of her life. Her mother was too busy making ends meet to see to her emotional needs.

When Serene was 13 years old, she started playing truant in school. She picked up smoking and hung out with gangs. She vandalised, stole and got involved in fights. These were thrilling experiences for her and she did not feel that anyone would care about what she did anyway. She started to engage in sexual activities with different men as that helped her to feel loved. Eventually, Serene became pregnant and had an abortion. Unable to control Serene, her parents eventually lodged a Beyond Parental Control complaint with the Juvenile Court and Serene was subsequently sent to the Singapore Girls' Home.

IS DIVORCE THE BEST OPTION?

PART 4

Contemplating a divorce is often a heart-wrenching and soul-searching experience. Many factors have to be considered when an adult thinks about divorce. These factors include having to make and adapt to changes, and new and uncertain challenges ahead. It is worse when there are children in the marriage. Even after making the decision to divorce, some adults tend to waver.

4.1 WHO SHOULD MAKE THE DECISION TO DIVORCE?

The decision of whether or not to divorce should be made by the couple. It should not be made for them by others such as friends, relatives or their children.

An adult should seriously contemplate the pros and cons of remaining in the marriage as opposed to leaving it. Divorce should not be an impulsive decision, as it may not spell the end to one's problems in life. In fact, divorce certainly requires making changes and meeting new challenges such as moving house, having to work longer hours to make ends meet or lowering one's living standard. It is good to talk to an impartial trusted friend, relative or professional counsellor who can look at the factors more objectively and guide you along. However, ultimately, the one contemplating divorce should make the important decision.

Before rushing into a divorce, it is useful to consider if marriage counselling will help to heal the rift in the marriage. Contrary to popular opinion, it is perfectly normal to seek counselling, whether for help with resolving one's personal issues or for problems related to the marriage, family or children. Marriage counselling may help to resolve the marital problems, especially if both partners are willing to make the effort to work things out.

Sometimes, there is persistent abuse of a spouse or the children, with no prospect of change on the part of the abusive spouse. In such cases, divorce may be the best option for the victims of such unhappy and dangerous relationships. Parents may be caught in a dilemma of wanting to preserve the family unit vs the need to protect their children from further abuse. Again, all the relevant facts should considered before a decision is made.

4.2 WHAT ARE THE LONG-TERM EFFECTS OF DIVORCE ON CHILDREN?

The effort that parents put in to help their children during and after a divorce plays a major role in determining whether their children can overcome the potentially detrimental effects of the divorce. Children with divorced parents face a greater likelihood of having a marital breakdown in adulthood compared with children from intact families. This could be due to the greater tendency for the child, as an adult, to fall into the same pattern of interaction with his spouse that he had witnessed between his parents.

In addition, some adults who had experienced in childhood their parents' separation may suffer from low self-esteem and rush into a marriage that they are ill-prepared for. Such adults may rush into a marriage to stave off feelings of rejection that they harbour following their parents' divorce.

Adults with divorced parents also have a greater tendency to 'solve' their marital difficulties in a maladaptive way. They may view divorce as an easier and more acceptable option out of a difficult relationship. These adults may be less tolerant of shortcomings in the marriage and less inclined to seek counselling.

There are, of course, adults with divorced parents who have healthy marriages. Some may even work harder on their marriages after having suffered the effects of divorce as children.

4.3   IS IT BETTER FOR ESTRANGED PARENTS TO STAY TOGETHER FOR THE 'SAKE OF THE CHILDREN'?

Children from intact but unhappy homes do not necessarily fare better than children with divorced parents. While such families may be intact, one or both parents may be emotionally distant from the children. Although children from divorced families may suffer a number of negative psychological effects, these can be minimised or avoided if their parents collaborate and allow healthy and regular contact between the non-custodial parent and the child.

Some children from divorced families report that while they do miss having both parents living together, they find more peace after their highly conflicted parents separate. Therefore, it is a myth that families are better off in staying together for the 'sake of the children', especially when parents fight constantly. It cannot be assumed that separation is the answer for all unhappily married parents or their children. Parents must consider if the pain of remaining married is greater than the pain of divorce. Most importantly, the safety of the parents and children should be the top priority when making this decision.

Parents who want a divorce should explain to their child that they are not giving up on the marriage because of the child, even if this were partly true. This shields the child from guilt and self-blame that can affect his self-esteem and emotional functioning. Assure the child that he is not the cause of the domestic conflict and could not have prevented it from happening. Assure him that although you will be separating from your spouse, both of you will still love and care for him.

4.4 I QUARREL WITH MY HUSBAND ALMOST EVERY DAY. SOMETIMES, MY HUSBAND WILL HIT ME IN FRONT OF OUR CHILDREN. WHAT ARE THE EFFECTS OF DOMESTIC VIOLENCE ON MY CHILDREN?

Usually, a child who witnesses fights, whether verbal or physical, responds with overwhelming fear for his safety and that of the abused parent. The experience can seriously damage the child's sense of security and control of his environment. If the child continues to be exposed to domestic violence, he may develop chronic anxiety and grow up with inaccurate and unhealthy ideas about dealing with relationships and conflict. He may think that it is acceptable to resort to violence and show abusive behaviour towards others, including his future spouse and children. On the other hand, some children may accept abuse as a norm, feel helpless and powerless and become victims of abuse themselves.

4.5 MY HUSBAND DOES NOT HAVE A REGULAR JOB, RARELY CONTRIBUTES FINANCIALLY AND OFTEN GETS DRUNK. WE QUARREL FREQUENTLY AND SOMETIMES VIOLENTLY. HOWEVER, HE DOES NOT WANT A DIVORCE. MY SON HAS STARTED GETTING INTO FIGHTS AND HIS GRADES HAVE SLIPPED. MY DAUGHTER HAS BECOME TIMID AND REFUSES TO GO TO SCHOOL. WHAT DO I DO?

Given the situation in your home, it is not surprising that your children are behaving as they do. Children who are affected by stressful events often do not verbalise their distress. Instead, they often act it out. This may include outbursts of rage, aggression and disruptive behaviour. Children who witness family violence may also become fearful, anxious and depressed.

It is common for children from chaotic families to lose interest in their studies. Your daughter may be refusing to go to school because she may be anxious about what will happen between her 'warring' parents if she were not at home. She may fear that her parents will seriously hurt each other during a fight.

Talk to your children about their fears and worries. You can also seek the help of a counsellor at their school or at a Family Service Centre. Your children may find it easier to share their fears and distress to someone outside the family. You should act quickly since both children appear to be very affected.

Finally, you and your husband could try marital counselling to help repair your relationship. Individual counselling for your husband will also help him to deal with his alcohol addiction. Even if your husband refuses, it is still useful for you to see a counsellor for your emotional well-being. If there is serious threat to your well-being and safety, you may want to quickly move yourself and your children to a place of safety, such as a women's shelter. If need be, get medical evidence of your physical injuries so that you can apply for a personal protection order against an abusive husband. A police report may also be required.

4.6   I AM IN A DILEMMA. I HAVE AN 8-YEAR-OLD DAUGHTER. MY HUSBAND IS A BAD-TEMPERED MAN WHO BEATS ME UP WHEN HE IS DRUNK. I HAVE ENDED UP IN HOSPITAL ON SEVERAL OCCASIONS. HE SOMETIMES BEATS MY DAUGHTER. I HAVE NO RELATIVES OR FRIENDS HERE AND AM WORRIED FOR MY CHILD AND MYSELF. SHOULD I GET A DIVORCE?

You have every right to live in safety and dignity and do not have to put up with spousal abuse, especially if you and your child are threatened. Your child deserves to be protected from abuse. If you are hurt, who will care for her? It is also frightening and emotionally unhealthy for children to witness violence at home.

Your first priority is to ensure that you and your child are safe from abuse. In Singapore, and in many other countries, spouses who have been physically abused can approach the Family Court for a personal protection order against the abusive spouse. The order can also be obtained on behalf of the child. The court will study the situation and decide if a personal protection order is required. In Singapore, the Child Protection Service of the Ministry of Social and Family Development will be called upon when there are complaints that a child below the age of 16 is being abused.

There are also organisations that provide temporary shelter to women and children who are victims of family violence. If you want to remain in the marriage, get your husband to go for counselling. There are Family Service Centres that provide counselling for men to overcome their violent behaviour. You and your spouse can also consider marital counselling. Part 10 of this book lists some places where you can get help. If you find it hard to talk to your husband, get someone whom he respects to talk to him instead. Whatever action you take, the foremost priority is the physical safety of you and your children.

BREAKING THE NEWS TO CHILDREN

PART 5

Some parents show little concern as to how their children feel about their divorce. They may mistakenly assume that young children will not understand anything about the situation. Also, parents may sometimes be struggling to manage their own feelings about the divorce and may not have the emotional resources to deal with their own pain and that of their children's. Divorce has a direct impact on children and they may suffer more mental repercussions if the situation is not clearly explained to them.

5.1   TO TELL OR NOT TO TELL?

It is essential for parents to discuss how they should prepare their children and inform them of their impending separation and divorce. This would minimise any needless guilt and self-blame that the children may experience (as Jeremy did in the case study below). Parents must anticipate their child's reactions and be prepared to tackle any questions the child may have.

CASE STUDY

TAKING THE BLAME

Seven-year-old Jeremy saw his parents quarrelling on the day he broke a glass of milk. He thought that his father was angry with him for his clumsiness and wrongfully concluded that his father left the home over the z milk incident. Jeremy felt dejected and was extremely guilty. He also blamed himself for causing his parents' separation and his mother's sadness. Wrecked by his immense sense of guilt, Jeremy could not concentrate on his studies and his grades fell.

5.2   HOW CAN I TELL MY CHILDREN ABOUT MY IMPENDING DIVORCE?

Most couples would have tried several methods to resolve their marital problems before deciding on a divorce. Inform your children about the divorce only when it is definite. Some parents tell the children that they are getting a divorce but later change their minds. Some parents threaten their spouses with a divorce but later change their minds. If parents are inconsistent and unsure, their children will begin to lose trust in them. Children are more likely to suffer more negative psychological effects from a divorce if they keep having parent-reunification fantasies.

Ideally, both parents should jointly and calmly explain to their child their intention to divorce. This lets the child know that he can rely on both his parents even if they separate. Having two parents for support and discussion helps to diminish any feelings of abandonment in the child. It also helps prevent him from blaming the absent parent for the break-up. The way children react to a divorce is related to how their parents inform them of it and how they treat each other post-divorce.

If you and your spouse cannot speak to each other calmly, then tell the child about the divorce separately. Try not to show your distress about the divorce to your child. Even if you are angry with your spouse, do not to speak ill of your spouse in front of your child. If you need to talk about your angry feelings concerning your ex-spouse, seek a friend or counsellor.

5.3   WHERE IS THE BEST PLACE TO BREAK THE NEWS OF OUR DIVORCE? WHEN IS THE BEST TIME?

The child may experience feelings of shock, fear, and disbelief when he hears the news of his parents' divorce. Therefore, you should break the news at home or in a familiar place where there will be no interruptions. Some children may get agitated or begin to cry, so it is important for them to be in a familiar place where they can feel comfortable enough to express their feelings. A teenager will probably wish to be left alone in his room to deal with his shock and grief. Parents must be sensitive to how the child feels when he hears the news and react in a supportive manner.

It is a grave mistake for parents to think that children will be less distressed if news of the divorce is broken to them at a restaurant, in a car or other public places.

You need to give the child time to absorb the news and adjust to the change. Ideally, allow at least a week between the news of the divorce and the parent's departure. This gives the non-custodial parent a chance to comfort the child and reaffirm future plans. Most importantly, this transition period helps to reduce the child's feelings of abandonment. On the other hand, allowing too much time to pass before the parent leaves only serves to deepen the child's denial of the divorce. He may start to think that the parent will not actually leave.

When breaking the news, parents should:
- arrange a proper time for a family meeting,
- plan ahead what to tell the children,
- remain cordial and calm,
- refrain from blaming each other or quarrelling,
- allow the children to ask questions,
- listen to their concerns seriously,
- make time to talk to the children after the session,
- reassure their children that they are still there for them even though the marriage is over.

5.4 MY DAUGHTER WILL BE STAYING WITH ME AFTER MY DIVORCE. SHE IS VERY CLOSE TO BOTH MY HUSBAND AND ME. EVEN NOW, SHE SOMETIMES PAINTS PICTURES OF US GETTING BACK TOGETHER. HOW CAN I BEST EXPLAIN THE SITUATION TO HER?

It is not uncommon for children, especially preschoolers and children at the lower primary level, to fantasise that their parents will reunite. Some of these fantasies may be verbalised as: "Mummy and Daddy are going to get married again" or "If I'm good, Mummy and Daddy will get back together."

Gently address your child's denial rather than scold her for harbouring such fantasies. Emphasise to your daughter that you have both tried to save the marriage but could not. However, do not badmouth her father even if he had contributed to the marital breakdown through his violence or marital infidelity. Explain to your child that the divorce is a result of difficulties between you and your husband, and that it is not her fault. Children are usually egocentric and naive and may assume that they are responsible for their parents' divorce.

5.5 MY HUSBAND AND I ARE GETTING A DIVORCE. HOW DO I BREAK THE NEWS TO MY YOUNG CHILDREN WITHOUT HURTING THEM? NEITHER OF US CAN BE CALM WITH THE OTHER AND WE BOTH DO NOT FEEL UP TO THE TASK. CAN WE GET SOMEONE ELSE TO TELL THE CHILDREN?

It is hard for parents to talk to their children about their divorce. It is an uncomfortable situation and strong emotions like anger, revenge and bitterness can emerge when couples talk about divorce. It is even harder for a parent, who is leaving the marriage for another partner, to talk to the children about the divorce, for fear of blame and guilt. It is not surprising that some parents wish to avoid the task altogether.

Yet, it is important for parents to talk to their child about their divorce. Unfortunately, parents may not always explain their intended divorce to their children in a helpful manner. They may benefit from having a close family member or friend present to assist them. Across cultures, issues like divorce may be handled differently.

If you and your husband cannot be civil to each other, it is best that each of you speak to the children separately. Be aware, however, that you should talk to the children when you are calm so that you do not end up criticising or blaming your partner, or breaking down badly. At the end of the day, it is essential for you to realise that your responsibility as a parent to your children remains even after the divorce. As your parenting journey continues even after the divorce, it would be particularly helpful for your children if both you and your ex-husband can maintain cordial ties with each other.

One important rule when telling children about a divorce is for parents to comfort the children and avoid making remarks that could directly or indirectly negatively influence their attitude towards the other parent. In fact, badmouthing the other parent can only alienate you from your child. The child's relationship and loyalty to either parent should remain intact even after the divorce. Keep in mind that the divorce is between you and your spouse, and not between the parents and the children.

5.6   MY SPOUSE HAD AN EXTRAMARITAL AFFAIR. HOW DO I EXPLAIN TO MY CHILDREN THE REASONS FOR DIVORCE?

As far as possible, children should be kept out of their parents' conflicts. Place your children's interests in a larger context by explaining that there are many reasons for the divorce and that both of you did try to work it out before deciding on a divorce. Explain the reason in a general manner. You can say, "Your father/mother and I cannot get along well. We are unhappy staying together. Therefore, we are separating. However, we are still your parents and will be there for you."

In this case, if you tell your children that the other parent is leaving because of his or her affair, this will affect their relationship with him or her in the future. Your children may become angry with the other parent for causing the family breakdown and it will be hard for them to outgrow this anger and maintain a good relationship with the other parent.

On the other hand, if the children already know about their parent's infidelity, it is better to refrain from further tarnishing your ex-spouse's image, no matter how tempting this is. By doing so, you are helping your children from becoming alienated from your ex-spouse. It is the errant parent's responsibility to explain his or her choices to the children.

Although a lot of parents are tempted to badmouth the straying parent and make the children take their side, it is best not cause alienation between the children and the errant parent. Instead, it is important to focus on other important matters, such as assuring your children of your love for them, informing them of the changes ahead and explaining upcoming plans regarding living arrangements or visitation schedule that you and your spouse have worked out. At this point of time, the important thing is to make sure that your children feel secure about the future.

5.7   MY HUSBAND HAS ABANDONED US FOR ANOTHER MARRIAGE. HE HAS MADE NO PLANS TO KEEP IN CONTACT WITH OUR DAUGHTER, WHO IS VERY CLOSE TO HIM. HOW SHOULD I HELP HER ACCEPT THE SITUATION?

The most essential task is to help your daughter emerge from the situation without feeling guilty, rejected or unloved. If your daughter does not receive visits or telephone calls from her father, she may think that she did something to drive him away and feel guilty and rejected. Reassure your child that her father's lack of communication is not her fault.

Now that your daughter has to depend on you for comfort, support and love, make sure that you do not lead her into thinking that her father is 'bad' as it will only lower her self-esteem. Help to ensure that your child is able to understand the difference between a person and their behaviour. A parent can still be a loving parent even if his or her behaviour may not be acceptable. Avoid communicating negative thoughts to your daughter about your ex-spouse, as it may negatively influence her perceptions of her father and affect her relationship with him.

Allow your child to vent her anger if she wants to. It would be helpful to create opportunities for your daughter to spend time with relatives or other adults who can support her through this period. Even if your daughter seems to have gotten over the situation, be sure to constantly monitor that she does not feel responsible for being abandoned by her father.

If possible, let your ex-husband know how his departure has led to serious psychological effects on your child. Try your best to convince him to have some, if not frequent, contact with your daughter. This may also take the form of short telephone calls or little cards he can send to her periodically. It is important for your ex-spouse to realise how important he is to your daughter.

5.8 MY MARRIAGE HAS BROKEN DOWN AND MY HUSBAND RECENTLY LEFT THE FAMILY. I THINK THAT MY 7-YEAR-OLD SON IS TOO YOUNG TO HANDLE THE TRUTH. SHOULD I LIE THAT HIS FATHER IS ON A BUSINESS TRIP?

Let's consider how feasible it may be to keep up with the story over an extended period of time. Over time, you would have to deal with your son's recurrent disappointment when his expectations of his father's return do not materialise. It may also be tiring for you to keep up with the lie. This may be more damaging than the truth, as your child may blame or be angry with you for hiding the truth from him when he eventually finds out.

Children will ultimately learn to accept their parents' separation. By withholding the truth, you are actually subjecting your son to more anxiety and uncertainty about his missing father. In addition, you risk having him regard you as an untrustworthy person and end up not trusting you. The sooner your son learns the truth, the earlier he can come to terms with the separation, resolve it and move on.

There is no specific age at which children are less affected by news of their parents' separation. The impact that such news will have on them is strongly influenced by the way parents break the news, and the affection and sensitivity they show the children during and after the divorce period. Any child who is capable of recognising the absence of a parent and is asking about that parent should be informed of the separation in a gentle and empathic manner.

CUSTODY AND ACCESS ISSUES

PART 6

For some children, visitation can be a happy and eagerly anticipated event. For others, it is a painful experience when they have to witness their parents quarrelling. In some cases, the visitation is accompanied by ugly fights and dramatic outbursts of anger and aggression between the maternal and paternal sides of the family. It is extremely important that parents remain objective and impartial to each other when dealing with matters concerning their children. If parents are unable to co-operate and be civil to each other, it is hard for the child to gain optimal benefits from his parent's visits. In such situations, the child may end up experiencing much anxiety about the access and display behavioural and psychological ill effects.

In Singapore, the Child Focused Resolution Centre (CFRC) was set up in 2011 by the then-Family Court (now Family Justice Courts) to support parents undergoing divorce so that these parents can focus on their child's needs and reach an agreement on the child's best care arrangements.

Refer to the following link for more information on the CFRC: www.familyjusticecourts.gov.sg/Common/Pages/MediationCounselling.aspx

6.1   WHAT ARE THE DIFFERENT TYPES OF CUSTODIAL CARE?

Parents undergoing divorce would have to discuss and agree on the two aspects:
- Custody – which parent(s) to make important decisions for child in the areas of medical, education and religion,
- Care and Control – which parent the child would live with, as well as provide support for child's day-to-day activities.

There are three types of custody arrangement:
- Sole custody – one parent will take care of the child and make all the decisions related to him,
- Joint custody – both parents will make the important decisions together, such as the choice of school, healthcare and his religious orientation,
- Split custody – when there is more than one child, the children may be divided between the two parents and each parent is responsible for a particular child. This is not a common custody arrangement.

If one parent consents to letting the other parent have custody of the children, then there will be no legal suit. If both parents want to have custody of the children, then each will have to present to the court his or her reasons for wanting custody, his or her ability to look after the child and the proposed parenting plan. The judge will consider several factors before deciding on who the more suitable candidate is. These factors include:

- the child's age and needs,
- the child's attachment to each parent, including grandparents or important caregivers,
- the amount of time each parent can commit to the child,
- each parent's physical and mental health,
- each parent's psychosocial background,
- any history of abuse or neglect by the parents.

Sometimes, the court may request that a court counsellor perform a custody and access evaluation to help with custody and access issues. The court's eventual custody order prioritises the child's best interests in terms of his emotional and physical well-being, safety and need for stability.

Sometimes, an interim custody and access order is issued until the actual custody and access decision is made. A visitation arrangement is also passed to dictate when, where and how often the children will see or stay with the non-custodial parent. To find out more about legal proceedings regarding divorce and child matters, you can check out the Family Justice Courts website.

6.2   MY WIFE AND I DIVORCED AFTER 10 YEARS OF MARRIAGE. I AM NOW FIGHTING FOR CUSTODY OF MY CHILDREN. I THINK THAT I AM IN A BETTER POSITION TO PROVIDE FOR THEM AS I EARN MORE, ALTHOUGH MY EX-WIFE HAS ALWAYS BEEN THE MAIN CAREGIVER. I AM WILLING TO SPEND TO ENSURE THAT I WIN THE CUSTODY SUIT. I PLAN TO GET A DOMESTIC HELPER TO LOOK AFTER THEM WHEN I AM AT WORK. IS THIS A GOOD ARRANGEMENT?

Although the children often develop bonds with both parents, they are usually close to their main caregiver, usually the mother. When parents separate, they should avoid unnecessary 'battles' over the children unless one parent has been abusive to them.

In your case, your children's main caregiver has always been their mother and the children are likely to have developed strong bonds with her. Disrupting the children's bonds with their mother may add to the trauma that your children already face because of the divorce. To ease the pain of a traumatic event and help children adapt positively, it is important to keep changes in their routines to a minimum. This means that it is better for them to stay with their mother, their secure base, and preferably in the same house as before.

Do consider the well-being of your children before plunging into a custody battle that is going to be emotionally and financially draining. It is better to channel your resources and energy into helping your children cope with the divorce and the changes that come with it. While a domestic helper may be able to provide the day-to-day care of the children, you should consider if your children's emotional, psychological or even spiritual needs could be better met by their mother. It is important to bear in mind that families do keep changing their domestic helpers and this is not good for the children if the helpers are their main caregivers. Generally, domestic helpers do not have the same sense of commitment towards their young charges, unlike the children's parents. Some helpers have also been caught abusing their young charges.

Nowadays, divorcing parents are encouraged to attend counselling sessions, run by the Family Court counsellors, that help parents understand and better deal with the impact of divorce on their children. It is hoped that the counselling sessions will help divorcing parents put aside their anger and hostility and focus on helping their children cope better with the trauma of a family breakdown.

Divorcing parents can try to resolve their custody and access matters amicably with the help of trained lawyers and other professionals via mediation or the collaborative family law approach, thereby avoiding an acrimonious, expensive and emotionally draining litigation route.

6.3   ARE VISITATION/ACCESS PRIVILEGES REALLY IMPORTANT? MY EX-HUSBAND HAD AN AFFAIR AND IS NOW LIVING WITH A NEW PARTNER. MY CHILDREN ARE DISTRESSED ABOUT LOSING HIM BUT I DO NOT WANT THEM TO INTERACT WITH HIM AS I THINK HE IS UNFIT TO BE A PARENT. AM I RIGHT IN THINKING THIS WAY?

No matter what you feel towards your ex-husband, do not let it get in the way of doing what is right for the children. Your children should have the chance to love their father and see him regularly. Every child from a divorced family needs to foster a strong and consistent relationship with both parents, unless there has been abuse. The end of your marriage does not signify the end of your children's relationship with their father. If a child is denied visitation privileges with the other parent, he may believe that this parent no longer loves him. This can intensify the child's existing sense of abandonment that he had been feeling as a result of his father's departure.

A child understands that he has traits from both parents. Therefore, if one parent is labelled as 'bad', the child may also see himself as being 'bad'. This psychological disturbance may lead to low self-esteem. Such a disturbed state of mind can adversely affect the child's academic and social performance.

You may think that by refusing your ex-husband access to your children, you are punishing your ex-husband. In reality, it is the children who get hurt, as they still love their father. Children will benefit from having a good relationship with both parents, wherever possible. Parents should always separate issues concerning their children from the issue of the divorce itself. As children have very strong loyalty instincts, seeing their parents being hostile to each other will only make them feel more miserable. Such children will often be at the losing end as they are constantly in the shadow of their parents' divorce.

To help your children grow up happily in a single-parent family, it is important to encourage them to have frequent contact with their father, if appropriate. Because of loyalty conflicts and fear of 'offending' their custodial parent, some children may outwardly indicate that they dislike being with the other parent. However, inwardly, they may yearn for the other parent and feel sad. Therefore, it will help if you give your children permission to love their father and maintain contact with him. In addition, when your children are with their father, you can have a well-deserved break to recharge your own batteries.

6.4   MY EX-WIFE DOES NOT ALLOW ME TO HAVE OVERNIGHT ACCESS TO MY 2-YEAR-OLD DAUGHTER, SO I SEE HER ONLY FOR FOUR HOURS EACH SATURDAY. SINCE I SPEND SO LITTLE TIME WITH HER, I THINK I SHOULD REDUCE THE AMOUNT I GIVE FOR HER MAINTENANCE. AFTER ALL, SINCE HER MOTHER USED TO HAVE A CAREER, SHE SHOULD RETURN TO WORK AND SUPPORT OUR DAUGHTER. AM I RIGHT?

You love your daughter and want to spend more time with her. It is also natural then for you to desire the best for your daughter, and this includes ensuring that her financial needs are adequately provided for. Your duty to provide for your daughter financially continues whether or not you are still married to her mother. Divorce does not change your paternal duty. Therefore, it is not advisable for you to peg your maintenance amount to the number of hours you have access to your child, as these are two separate issues.

Many non-custodial parents often make the mistake of not providing enough financially for their children after the divorce. Some do it to 'take revenge' on their ex-spouses. Ultimately, however, it is the children who suffer from the decreased amount of maintenance. This is unfair to the children as they are not responsible for their parents' divorce. Remember too that as your daughter grows up, her financial needs will increase correspondingly and you will have to adjust your monetary contribution accordingly.

Furthermore, your daughter is still very young and has been looked after by her mother since her birth. At this stage, when your daughter is going through the trauma of her parents' divorce and the associated lifestyle changes, she will be feeling rather insecure. At this point, your daughter needs her mother's presence, attention and care more than ever before. If your ex-wife is forced to work because of reduced finances from you, it is your daughter who will suffer. In the event that mother has to return to work, it is important to financially support suitable care arrangements for your child.

You remain responsible towards the reasonable upkeep of your daughter, even after your marriage has ended.

6.5 MY HUSBAND AND I DIVORCED BECAUSE HE HAS A SERIOUS MENTAL ILLNESS AND REQUIRES FREQUENT HOSPITALISATIONS. MY HUSBAND CAN TURN VIOLENT AND IRRATIONAL WHEN HE IS UNWELL. HE IS NOT COMPLETELY STABLE BETWEEN HIS PERIODS OF ILLNESS BUT HE LOVES OUR 4-YEAR-OLD SON AND WANTS TO SEE HIM REGULARLY. SHOULD HE HAVE ACCESS TO HIS SON?

Mental illness alone does not make your ex-husband unsuited to have access. The more important issue is the child's safety and well-being when in your ex-husband's care. For your son's safety, he should not see his father when his father is unwell. It can also be quite frightening for your young son to see his father in a disturbed mental state. A better option is to have a relative or neutral party such as a counsellor to supervise the access, either voluntarily or through a court order. Despite his mental illness, your ex-husband seems to care for his son and deserves reasonable regular access to him.

6.6   MY 7-YEAR-OLD DAUGHTER USED TO LOVE HER FATHER DEARLY. NOW, SHE THROWS TERRIBLE TANTRUMS WHEN HE COMES FOR HER. SOMETIMES, SHE WILL CALM DOWN AND GO TO HIM. SHOULD SHE STOP SEEING HER FATHER ALTOGETHER? EVEN THOUGH I DON'T HAVE ANY POSITIVE FEELINGS FOR MY EX-HUSBAND, I KNOW THAT HE LOVES MY DAUGHTER AND WOULD BE DOING HIS BEST TO MEET HER NEEDS DURING ACCESS.

Your daughter's tantrums could be due to several reasons, such as:
- the stress of the divorce itself,
- the trauma of being separated from the main caregiver,
- the anxiety of adapting to a new place and routine,
- her perception that she should be loyal to only one parent,
- her irrational fear that she may not see you again after she goes for visitation.

When your child is with her father, she may be have mixed feelings. This happens especially if she knows or thinks that her parents dislike each other. Your daughter may think that you will feel hurt if she seems too happy to see her father. This may be causing her to downplay or hide her joy about seeing her father in an attempt to prevent you from feeling threatened or disappointed.

Sometimes, a child may worry about the well-being of the custodial parent who is left alone at home. The child may feel the same way about the non-custodial parent when he or she has to leave the non-custodial parent. Whatever the reason, do not terminate your husband's access privileges as this may lead your daughter to think that her father does not love her. Consequently, this may cause the child to feel rejected and doubt her self-worth.

Where possible, encourage your ex-husband to be patient with your daughter, talk to her gently and show her that his love for her is unconditional. Refrain from shouting at your daughter or dragging her away as this can be traumatic for her. Your ex-husband may have to start with short outings and gradually increase the duration. On your part, think about the signals that you send when your husband comes for her. Children are much attuned to their environment. If you seem unhappy, your daughter may blame herself for upsetting you. She may then refuse to leave with her father for fear that you will be unhappy.

It is important for your daughter to know that she has your total approval and permission to be with her father. You can help your daughter by telling her to enjoy her time with her father, and to tell you all about it when she comes back. Doing this will help your daughter to be less ambivalent about the visits and her tantrums should reduce over time. You can also let your daughter know that you will be meaningfully occupied while she is away so that she does not worry about abandoning you at home.

Some custodial parents forbid their children to talk positively about the other parent. This should be avoided as it gives rise to feelings of guilt in the children.

In some cases, some children show disturbed behaviour when it is time for access. Further analysis usually shows that this is the result of the child witnessing the parents or extended families fighting physically or quarrelling nastily during an unpleasant handover. The child's reluctance to follow the non-custodial parent is often due to the adults' often-unreasonable behaviours inducing needless fear and conflicts in the child. In reality, the child may actually be willing to see the other parent if not for the unpleasant and frightening encounter between the 'warring' parties. Such children and parents need counselling and will benefit from access supervised by external and neutral professionals.

6.7 I AM GRANTED ACCESS ON SATURDAYS TO MY TEENAGE SON. HOWEVER, HE PREFERS TO SPEND HIS TIME ON SCHOOL ACTIVITIES OR WITH HIS FRIENDS. THIS UPSETS ME A LOT AND WE, HIS PARENTS, HAVE QUARRELLED OVER THE MATTER A FEW TIMES. AS I HAVE ONLY WEEKLY ACCESS TO HIM, I CONSIDER EVERY MOMENT TO BE PRECIOUS. HOWEVER, I AM NOT SURE HE FEELS THE SAME WAY AS I DO. SHOULD I STRICTLY ENFORCE THE VISITATION SCHEDULE OR ALLOW HIM TO DO WHAT HE WANTS?

You are going to risk putting a strain on your relationship with your son if you insist on following a fixed schedule. As children enter into adolescence, their need to be with friends and having their own social lives becomes more important than spending time with family members.

Teenagers are striving for independence and an identity of their own. They also have more commitments compared to when they were younger. Now that your son is a teenager, he has to split his limited time between school, homework, friends, extra-curricular activities, family and you. It may be wiser for you to negotiate with your son and try to work out a schedule that can accommodate his and your needs. Doing this allows for a win-win situation for both of you.

Parents with adolescent children should practice reasonable flexibility. It is unrealistic to set a rigid schedule for teenagers. If your son insists that he has to miss a particular weekend with you, do not push the point. Instead, show interest in what he is doing and at the same time, gently highlight to him that you would really love to spend time doing something with him. Try to work out an alternate schedule, for example, a quick dinner on a weekday. It is okay not to spend the same number of hours together each week. What is more important is the quality of the time that you have with him. Allowing space for negotiation will reduce the tension between both of you and make your time together more enjoyable.

6.8 AFTER MY DIVORCE, I WAS GIVEN WEEKLY ACCESS TO MY SON. THE BOND BETWEEN US IS NOT VERY STRONG AS I USED TO TRAVEL FREQUENTLY. HE WOULD SCREAM AND BE EMOTIONALLY DISTRESSED WHEN IT WAS TIME FOR ME TO PICK HIM UP. THE COURT DECIDED THAT I SHOULD NOT HAVE ANY ACCESS TO HIM UNTIL HE IS OLDER AND BETTER ABLE TO HANDLE THE SITUATION. I AM AFRAID THAT HE WILL FORGET ME. WHAT DO I DO?

Certain children get very worked up and feel traumatised when they are forced to see the non-custodial parent. Despite counselling, they still suffer great distress when meeting the parent.

In such circumstances, it is better for the non-custodial parent to stay away for a while for the sake of the child.

During this period, you can still keep in touch with your child through short and pleasant telephone calls, letters, birthday gifts or taped audio messages. Even if he does not reciprocate, continue to patiently show your care for him. You can also ask your spouse to encourage your son to have better relations with you. You and your spouse should try to relate with each other amicably, despite any bitter past experiences or feelings, as that will help your son look at access more positively.

In some cases, counselling for you, your son and your ex-spouse may help to smooth the access process. A graduated, supervised access with the help of neutral counsellors will be helpful.

6.9 I HAVE WEEKLY ACCESS TO MY DAUGHTER WHO LIVES WITH MY EX-WIFE. WHEN I PICK HER UP, INVARIABLY, THERE ARE HARSH WORDS EXCHANGED BETWEEN MY EX-WIFE AND MYSELF. MY DAUGHTER IS BEGINNING TO THROW HER TEMPER AND HIT US. THIS BEHAVIOUR HAS NOT STOPPED DESPITE MY TALKING TO HER ABOUT IT. HOW DO I STOP THIS?

Children can experience anger, guilt, sadness and fear when their parents quarrel. The feelings can intensify if the parents pressure their children to take sides. Such negative parental behaviour can also deeply wound and confuse the children who feel trapped between their parents.

Both of you should avoid raising your voices, becoming angry or passing insulting or threatening remarks in front of your daughter. If you have conflicts with your ex-wife over maintenance fees, parenting issues or visitation problems, discuss them in private. When the two of you quarrel in front of your daughter, in addition to frightening her, both of you are setting a bad example on how conflicts should be resolved. Resolving conflicts amicably with the goal of finding solutions will set a better example for your daughter than senseless quarrelling.

Parents may sometimes find it hard to speak cordially to their ex-spouse due to unresolved issues from the divorce or disagreement on issues of parenting or maintenance. To the child, witnessing parental fights can be a rather terrifying and bitter experience. The emotional distress that children feel is usually manifested in the form of behavioural problems. Your daughter's behaviour may be her way of coping with the post-divorce pain she feels when she sees both of you fight. As far as possible, try to minimise friction when you meet your ex-wife.

Some parents may think that the child is throwing a tantrum to take advantage of the tension between her parents and get her own way. However, the child's tantrums may actually be the result of her unspeakable distress about her parental conflicts. By being civil and cooperative with each other, parents can help to minimise their child's emotional distress.

A point to note is that sometimes a child's temper tantrums may be a plea to be heard. Often divorced parents with ongoing conflicts are so caught up with 'taking revenge' on each other that they fail to notice their child's needs and distress. Check if your daughter is using tantrums to get both your attention. If so, give your daughter regular attention so that she need not use negative behaviours to meet her legitimate need for love and attention. You may not have been able to protect your daughter from the pain of divorce, but you can minimise further psychological damage by being civil and cooperative with your ex-wife.

6.10 MY HUSBAND FREQUENTLY GOES BACK ON HIS WORD REGARDING VISITATIONS. HE FAILS TO TURN UP, WITHOUT INFORMING US, ALTHOUGH MY SON IS EAGERLY ANTICIPATING HIS ARRIVAL. AT OTHER TIMES, HE DEMANDS ACCESS TO MY SON AT SHORT NOTICE. WILL THIS HAVE AN IMPACT ON MY SON?

Every child wants to spend time with each of his parents, so it must be disappointing when your son is kept waiting to see his father who does not turn up. If this happens repeatedly, your son will think that his father is not committed to him and he is likely to feel neglected and rejected. The feeling of rejection may cause your son to feel inferior about himself and damage his trust in his father. On the other hand, springing surprise visits is just as bad as such visits may be confusing to him and disrupt his routine and schedules.

It is important for your ex-husband to be aware of how his inconsistent visits can affect your son negatively. Parents need to understand that keeping to routines and scheduled visits helps to build trust and security in a child's life.

When your ex-husband is unable to keep to his visits, remind him to call your son and explain his reasons clearly. Your son needs to be assured that he is not being neglected. If your ex-husband needs to postpone his visit, tell him to inform you a few days in advance. Constantly check with your son to see how he feels about being unable to see his father.

If your ex-husband fails to turn up for visitation, you can soothe your son's disappointment by engaging him in alternative activities to keep him occupied.

6.11 I HAVE SPECIFIC RULES IN MY HOME AND MY CHILDREN ARE GENERALLY OBEDIENT. HOWEVER, WHEN THEY ARE WITH THEIR FATHER ON WEEKENDS, ALL THEY DO IS WATCH MOVIES AND PLAY ARCADE GAMES, WITH THE RESULT THAT THEIR HOMEWORK IS LEFT UNFINISHED. ON MONDAYS, THEIR TEACHERS CALL TO

COMPLAIN THAT THEIR ASSIGNMENTS ARE NOT COMPLETED. WHAT SHOULD I TELL MY EX-HUSBAND?

It is good that your husband is still committed to the children despite the divorce and sees them regularly. While it is nice for them to go out on weekends, it is better if they have a more balanced life where there are treats as well as time for ordinary things such as cooking a meal, having a chat, playing boardgames and doing homework. Doing such activities will give them more time to communicate with their father, and they can also learn to be more disciplined. This also ensures that the children maintain routine in their lives, as otherwise it would be challenging for them to make weekly adjustments as they alternative between households.

Inform your ex-husband about the teachers' complaints in a calm manner. Discuss with him ways in which the children can balance their time between homework and leisure time. Try your best to convey the message in a non-confrontational way so that your ex-husband does not become defensive and uncooperative.

6.12 I SUSPECT MY EX-WIFE IS ABUSING OUR 8-YEAR-OLD DAUGHTER. MY DAUGHTER HAS GONE WITHOUT FOOD A FEW TIMES, AND ON SEVERAL VISITS, I HAVE SEEN HER BEING SCOLDED 'DUMB' AND 'UGLY'. THERE ARE ALSO BRUISES ON HER ARMS BUT WHEN I QUESTION HER MOTHER ABOUT THEM, SHE WAVES THEM OFF WITH FEEBLE EXCUSES. IF MY DAUGHTER IS AT RISK OF ABUSE, WHAT STEPS CAN I TAKE TO PROTECT HER?

A child who is repeatedly criticised and ridiculed will gradually believe that she is worthless and unloved. Over time, her self-image and self-esteem would be eroded. Repeatedly ignoring the needs of the child, blaming, threatening and belittling a child can be considered emotional abuse. Likewise, repeatedly sustaining physical injuries like multiple bruises, burns, cuts, fractures and black eyes may be evidence of physical abuse.

Every parent would want the best for his child. Usually, abusive parents are ignorant about the detrimental effects the child will suffer.

Sometimes because of inadequate parenting skills or having to deal with stressors in their life, such as struggling to earn a living or not having enough energy or rest, these parents resort to harsh but fast means to discipline the child. Unfortunately, their failure to understand that their methods are ineffective in the long run can have severe consequences on the child. Talk to your ex-spouse calmly about the way she handles her daughter. You can also:

- approach a mental health professional or a counsellor for family counselling as well as advice on effective parenting methods,
- take advantage of parenting workshops that are run by social service agencies,
- arrange for your daughter to speak with a counsellor to help her deal with her negative feelings.

If there are signs of physical or sexual abuse, take the child for an immediate medical examination. If the doctors find sufficient evidence of abuse, they will notify the relevant authorities (the police and child protection officers at the Ministry of Social and Family Development) who will then investigate further. You can also apply for a suspension of the current custodial arrangements via the court until the situation clears up.

6.13 MY HUSBAND DIVORCED ME TO MARRY ANOTHER WOMAN. PERHAPS BECAUSE HE FEELS GUILTY ABOUT IT, HE SPOILS MY SON DURING THEIR TIME TOGETHER. THE RESULT IS THAT MY SON HAS BECOME VERY DEMANDING. WHEN I REFUSE HIS UNREASONABLE REQUESTS, HE GETS ANGRY AND SAYS, "YOU ARE MEAN. DAD IS BETTER THAN YOU." SHOULD I GIVE IN TO HIM SO THAT I WILL NOT LOSE MY SON – THE ONLY THING LEFT IN THE WORLD FOR ME?

Your son's words can be hurtful but remember that as a responsible parent, you have to instil discipline and refuse his unreasonable demands, whether or not he likes it. If you do not, your son may grow up to be selfish and demanding after being used to having his way.

Stay calm and do not threaten to abandon him. Tell him firmly but politely that you cannot allow him to do get away with unreasonable demands or negative behaviour. Do not get into arguments about who is the better parent. Acknowledge your child's feelings and explain the rationale for your decision. This will let him understand your expectations and know that you love and care for him. It also spares unnecessary ugly scenes with him, which can damage your relationship.

If possible, try to tell your ex-husband in a calm way that it is important that your son has a healthy and balanced dose of love and discipline. Help him understand that spoiling your son is not going to help him develop into a mature and likeable person.

Do remember that you are an individual with value, whether you are married, single or divorced. As such, take care of yourself and avoid letting your child become the entire reason for your existence. You should venture out to make new, reliable friends and develop other useful interests such as taking up a hobby or a vocational course.

CASE STUDY

FINDING THE MIDDLE GROUND

Five-year-old Shani frequently complained of headaches and stomachaches. Her mother sent her for a check-up but there was nothing physically wrong with her. She was later referred to a psychiatrist for an assessment. Shani's parents had divorced about two years ago.

At the session, Shani drew an unhappy face to represent herself. She was encouraged to talk about her experiences of having access with her father. Being extremely attached to her mother, Shani indicated that she found it very difficult to leave her mother for her father. Every visit by her father was a traumatic event. He would accuse his ex-wife of influencing Shani not to go with him and often dragged her away from her mother.

Despite forcefully dragging a screaming Shani away from her mother, during the access, Shani's father would usually be spending time with his girlfriend in his room and leave Shani in the hands of the domestic helper. Shani's father would also not allow Shani to have telephone contact with her mother during the access.

Both parents were counselled about the way they were handling the access. They were informed that Shani felt rather traumatised and frightened by her parents' quarrels and fights during the access handover. Shani was particularly disturbed when her father forcibly pulled her away from her mother. She felt sad and angry that her father was not spending time with her during her access.

Shani's parents mutually agreed to carry out the access handover in the presence of a therapist. As there was no quarrelling or a dramatic and ugly scene between the parents, Shani felt safe and secure about interacting with her father. The supervised access gave them a chance to have a better relationship. It also gave the therapist a chance to model ways for her father to interact with Shani in a warm and nurturing manner. Shani's father also realised that he needed to spend personal time with Shani and not leave the emotional nurturing to his maid. He made an effort to spend individual time with Shani during the access. Eventually, Shani managed to have regular, overnight access with her father without any problems.

6.14 MY EX-HUSBAND TELLS MY CHILDREN LIES ABOUT ME WHEN HE HAS ACCESS TO THEM. WHAT SHOULD I DO?

Many parents do this in the hope of getting the children to take their side. However, children, who love both their parents, can often see through these lies and may start resenting the parent who is badmouthing the other. In your case, avoid badmouthing your ex-spouse, as that will only put your children in a difficult position. It is important for both parents to maintain their self-respect and respect for the other parent. This would model respectful behaviour to the child and help him cope better with the after-effects of divorce. Engage your ex-husband where possible and discuss calmly about how his actions are unhelpful for all concerned. Otherwise, get a neutral third party to explain the situation to your ex-husband.

6.15 MY EX-HUSBAND HAS ACCESS TO MY 5-YEAR-OLD DAUGHTER EVERY WEEKEND. HOWEVER, SHE STARTS SCREAMING THE MOMENT SHE SEES HER FATHER AND HIS PARENTS. WHEN SHE REFUSES TO GO OVER TO HIM, THEY WILL ACCUSE US OF POISONING HER MIND. HOW CAN I IMPROVE THE SITUATION?

Your daughter's reaction is hardly surprising. Having to leave you for her father's home is already stressful and the sight of seeing you quarrel can further frighten her. Her crying and distress can be significantly reduced if the adults around her handle the situation with more calm and civility. On your part, encourage your daughter to go with her father and give her a familiar toy or item to take with her. Also, be calm yourself. If you show distress or disapproval, it will be difficult for her to leave with her father.

On his part, your ex-husband and his family should stop accusing you and instead focus their energy on reassuring and comforting the child. If you have trouble talking to your ex-husband reasonably, get a neutral person to communicate the matter to him. Supervised access may also help your husband and your daughter to get used to each other, bond better and get over the issue.

CASE STUDY

NO REASON TO CHOOSE SIDES

Ryan, aged 12, moved out with his mother when she could no longer tolerate her husband scolding and hitting her. She wanted a divorce. Both parents wanted custody of Ryan. Ryan's mother often told him that his father was a bad husband because he abused her, treated her like a maid and did not contribute financially. Ryan felt uncomfortable hearing this, as he still loved his father.

Each time Ryan returned from his visits to his father, he would behave in a rebellious and defiant manner towards his mother, although he liked living with her. Ryan's parents were always pestering him to choose between them. Ryan felt lost and torn. He longed for both parents and felt guilty for taking sides. He started to behaved badly in school and failed all his subjects in the mid-term examinations. The school referred him to a counsellor.

During the individual counselling sessions, Ryan was encouraged to express his feelings. He was led to realise that he was still his parents' child despite the divorce and that he had the right to love them both. His parents were also educated on the importance of co-parenting instead of trying to run each other down.

Fortunately, Ryan's parents put aside their hostility, stopped badmouthing each other and focused on helping Ryan to move on. This helped Ryan stop his behavioural problems and pay attention to his studies.

6.16 WHENEVER MY EX-HUSBAND PICKS UP OUR THREE GIRLS, HE OFTEN STARTS A FIGHT WITH ME. HE WILL PASS SARCASTIC REMARKS ABOUT ME AND ACCUSE ME OF BEING IMMORAL. SOMETIMES, HE WILL EVEN INTERROGATE MY CHILDREN ON WHETHER OR NOT I AM DATING ANYONE. WHAT SHOULD I DO?

Avoid a scene in front of the children. There is no point in arguing with someone who is unwilling to listen and show you respect. When your ex-husband begins his tirade against you, it is best to avoid getting into a pointless argument. It may appear that you are backing off but it is a smart way not to get into a useless argument. If you continue like this, he will eventually stop his negative behaviour.

You can tell your children that they can politely inform their father that they do not know whether you are dating someone. Children should not be used as spies.

The purpose of access is for the non-custodial parent to enjoy the children's company and vice versa. When access becomes difficult, the affected parent can apply to court for the visitation period to be supervised by a neutral party, such as a counsellor, who could defuse the situation.

Points to remember

It is extremely important for a child to have an ongoing relationship with the non-custodial parent. There will be times when parents are unable to protect the child from the hurt associated with visitation disputes. Here are some helpful points to remember:

- Avoid passing unkind remarks or complaining about your ex-spouse. Parental conflict forces children to take sides, which often leaves them trapped in the middle. This is not necessary and unfair to the children.
- Talk to your children openly about their visitation experience but keep away from the subject of your ex-spouse's private affairs. Do not ask your children to share private information about the other parent.
- Make sure your children do not become messengers between you and your ex-spouse. Communicate with your ex-spouse directly on issues pertaining to school, visitation schedules, health and financial matters.
- Keep to a consistent visitation schedule to give children a sense of security and stability.
- Do not let children make visitation decisions. Some parents allow children to refuse visitations and decide on the schedule, but they

may be too young to understand the importance of maintaining a relationship with their non-custodial parent. Take charge and implement a consistent visitation schedule. If your children are teenagers, you can discuss alternative schedules with them. Be firm on the duration of the visits. Some children manipulate their parents to get their way, such as returning home later than expected to avoid doing homework. Children need to know that parents are in control and that there are rules they must obey.

- If you are the non-custodial parent, you should keep to the visitation schedule and not show up without notice. Doing so is disruptive and may clash with your child's routine. For young children, the transition from one parent to the other will pose some difficulty. They should be given enough time to mentally and emotionally prepare to part with their main caregiver. Do not miss or reschedule visits unless absolutely necessary. This minimises the chance of conflict with your ex-spouse.

- If the child is very young and is having overnight access with one parent, allow him to telephone his main caregiver parent if he wants. This will help him to feel more secure and enjoy his access time.

- During access, spend time with the child and do not relegate his care to your domestic helper or some other caregiver, unless you have some important or urgent matter to attend to. The purpose of the access is to build your relationship with your child. So, take the effort and time to nurture your child and the relationship. Remember that the bonds you build with your child when he is young will determine how he relates to you as an adult. Unfortunately, there are parents who fight tooth and nail over access for the sake of 'taking revenge' on their ex-spouse and then neglect the child during access. This will backfire on you when you, the parent, grow older and look to your child for physical, emotional or financial support.

- Do not tie your financial contribution for your child's upkeep to the amount of access you are allowed to have with your child. Some parents, especially non-custodial fathers, withhold or give irregular or inadequate child support to spite their ex-wives. This is wrong, as it will deprive your child of the financial means necessary for essential expenses like school and tuition fees, food, clothing and shelter.

DATING AFTER DIVORCE

PART 7

No matter how difficult a marriage or divorce is, the wounds of the divorce will heal over time. More often than not, each parent will move on to start dating again and explore a possible long-term relationship with another partner. When parents start dating, it has significant meaning for the children, no matter how old they are. Seeing their parent with a new partner means that the children's lingering fantasy of having their parents reunite is dashed. Also, they must now 'share' their parent with another person. Some children may even start to fear that they may be ignored if their parents remarry and have children from the new marriage.

7.1 WHEN IS THE RIGHT TIME FOR A DIVORCED PARENT TO START DATING?

Children are usually traumatised by a divorce in the family and they need time to adjust to a new situation. The time needed to accept the divorce and overcome the hurt varies from one child to another. Some children continue having issues regarding their family break-up even after they become adolescents or adults. The impact of their parents' break-up may resurface when the parents start dating. It may be helpful if divorced parents let their children know (in age-appropriate language) that they will be developing new relationships. Children will adjust better to parents' new partners when they feel reassured of their parents' love.

7.2 HOW ARE CHILDREN AFFECTED WHEN THEIR PARENTS START DATING?

When a parent starts dating, the child sees it as confirmation that his parents are not going to get together again. The child may react angrily to the parent, but more often this anger will be directed at the parent's new partner. The child may be more irritable in front of the partner or simply retreat to his bedroom to show his displeasure. His anger may take the form of jealousy because he now has to share the parent's time with the new partner.

Children do not understand that the relationship between parent and child is different from that between a dating couple. To children, loving one person means that you cannot love another. Their naivety may leave them feeling inadequate about themselves and in doubt about their parent's love for them. Furthermore, when a parent is conspicuously affectionate to his date, the child may feel that he is not as valuable as the date. The child may develop a sense of insecurity as he imagines that the parent may leave him for good in favour of the new date.

Some teenagers may feel awkward about their parent's open display of affection towards someone of the opposite sex. It is difficult and embarrassing for them to accept that their parent will be sexually active with another person.

Not all children, however, disapprove of their parents' new partners. Some children may encourage it as they stand to benefit if there are fun-filled family outings as well as additional love and attention for them. If the child forms a nurturing and loving relationship with the date, he will feel protected and safe.

Normally, children who have successfully come to terms with their parents' divorce are more accepting of their parents' new relationships. Adolescents may also react better when a parent starts dating because they are in the process of distancing themselves from their family and identifying more with their peers. They may be relieved that their parent has someone else to rely on for support and companionship.

7.3   I GOT DIVORCED A YEAR AGO. WHILE I AM NOT YET READY TO SETTLE DOWN WITH ANYONE, I HAVE BEEN DATING REGULARLY. WILL THIS HAVE AN IMPACT ON MY CHILDREN?

There are children who form attachments to their parent's new dates fairly easily. This is especially the case with younger children, who respond well to friendliness, gifts, outings and fun activities with their parents and their dates.

Parents should understand that when a child forms an attachment to the new date, he may feel hurt when his parent's special relationship with this person ends. To the child, the experience may be similar to losing a parent to a divorce. The child may then view the world as being unreliable, insecure and untrustworthy. Parents should preferably avoid engaging in serial dating sprees. Parents need to find a balance between being open about their new relationships and protecting the child until the parent is ready to commit to a new relationship. Protecting the child from over-exposure to the parent's dating activities would be in the best interest of the child.

7.4   I REALLY LIKE MY NEW GIRLFRIEND. YET, MY CHILDREN ARE HOSTILE AND MAKE THINGS DIFFICULT FOR HER. HOW CAN I GET THEM TO ACCEPT HER?

Listen to your children's thoughts and feelings about the situation and find out what their fears and worries are. Be open to hear what it is about your new girlfriend that upsets them. It may be difficult for the children to talk about their feelings, as they may fear that you may get angry. However, it is important for you to clarify what the exact reason is behind their behaviour and do something helpful about it.

Children can sometimes be blind to their feelings. Once they form a bad impression of your date, they can find countless reasons not to like her. By listening to them without immediately jumping to your girlfriend's defence, you can demonstrate that you respect their views. Take the opportunity to assure them that they will always have a special place in your heart.

Let your children build a relationship with your new girlfriend at their own pace. Do not hurry them. They may feel that they are betraying their mother by accepting the new person, and this may increase their resistance to getting to know her.

Avoid over-emphasising on your new partner's good qualities as the children may feel that you are only on her side. Also, encourage your girlfriend to show them consistent affection even if they initially react negatively to her.

Be sensitive to how your children feel when you are with your girlfriend.

Are you demonstrating too much affection and physical intimacy by hugging, kissing and caressing her in front of your children?

Are you giving all your attention to your girlfriend when the family is together?

If this is the case, then the children are most likely to be threatened by your girlfriend's presence. Minimise these tendencies with your girlfriend until your children feel at ease with her. Continue to give them attention and love even though you now have an additional interest in your life.

Important things for parents to note if they are dating

- Refrain from engaging in overt displays of affection with your dates in the presence of their children. Be aware that you may do so unconsciously because of the excitement of a new partner.
- Do not use the date as a stand-in parent in your absence. The date has no right to discipline the children on a parent's behalf.
- Be discerning about bringing the date home for overnight stays. Consider the feelings of your children and their receptivity towards the new date. Having a date stay over may also have an impact on the children's moral development and erode the parent's authority

in instilling moral values in his children, especially when they are adolescents.

- Do not engage in overtly sexual activities in front of the children; this may be considered child sexual abuse. Parents should take care not to expose children to any sexual activities.
- Do not use your children to spy on the love affairs of your ex-spouse. Children should never be probed for information about the other parent's love life.
- Ensure that you give time and attention to your children even if you have a new love interest. Some parents make the mistake of neglecting their children when they are with their new partner.

CASE STUDY

THE JEALOUS CHILD

Fifteen-year-old Mei Mei was upset to see a woman sitting beside her father when his car pulled up in front of the school. In the car, she noticed her father laughing merrily at his date's jokes. He had obviously been late in picking her up because he had gone out with the woman. Mei Mei could sense that the woman was not her father's usual business acquaintance. His attention was totally on his girlfriend during the car ride. To make matters worse, he even invited her to have dinner with them. Mei Mei could feel a sense of jealousy surging within her. She felt threatened and insecure.

At home, Mei Mei became hostile and started a quarrel with her father over petty things. When they cooled down, they had a heart-to-heart talk. Her father realised that Mei Mei was unhappy over the way he had behaved with his girlfriend and the fact that he had ignored her in the car. He explained to Mei Mei that he had begun dating again. He then made the effort to spend some time alone with her. His actions helped to comfort Mei Mei and affirmed that her father still loved her. Gradually, Mei Mei became more understanding and began to interact positively with her father's girlfriend.

REMARRIAGE AND STEP-FAMILIES

PART 8

Some children are happier in step-families, especially if their step-parent gives them better supervision and care than their biological parent ever did. However, there are new issues that the family members may have to face. If a dating relationship is leading to a marriage, a parent should gradually introduce his new partner into his children's lives. If possible, the children should also be introduced to prospective relatives, including future step-siblings.

Parents need to anticipate their children's reactions towards a new step-parent and the latter's role in the family. The step-parent should bear in mind that he should not try to be a substitute for the child's biological parent. The transition to a new family is difficult for everyone, especially for children who may have suffered considerably from their parents' divorce.

8.1   HOW DOES A SECOND MARRIAGE AFFECT THE CHILDREN?

Many children may become stressed when their custodial parent remarries. First, it destroys their fantasies about their parents getting back together eventually. Also, the parent may give the child less time and attention. So, instead of feeling that they have gained a step-parent, the children may feel that they have lost yet another parent. Furthermore, if remarriage means a new home, new school, and new relatives, the children have additional adjustments and issues to deal with.

As with any kind of disruption to their lives, do not be surprised if children become angry and argumentative, get into fights, show disobedience or lose concentration in their studies. Loyalty conflict is often the most disturbing issue for children. Some children try to harden themselves against having positive feelings about the step-parent. Otherwise, they may feel that they are betraying their non-custodial parent.

Preparing children for a new family

- Inform them of the changes that will come with your remarriage.
- Discuss the remarriage with them – children are eager to know the answers to questions such as "Where will I stay?", "Can I still study in my school?", "Can I still see my other parent?", "What do I call my step-parent?"
- Give them lots of assurance that they are still your children and you will still love them.

- Remind them that they will still keep regular contact with the non-custodial parent. Assure them that the step-parent would never replace the role of their biological parent.
- Make sure that you continue to spend time with your children even when you have a new spouse or other children through your new marriage.

8.2 MY NEW WIFE HAS A SON FROM HER PREVIOUS MARRIAGE. IT IS HARD FOR ME TO COMMUNICATE WITH HIM. HE SAYS THINGS LIKE "YOU ARE NOT MY REAL FATHER. WHY SHOULD I LISTEN TO YOU?" HOW CAN I HAVE A REAL FATHER-SON RELATIONSHIP WITH HIM?

Children seldom view a step-parent as a real parent as they usually maintain strong loyalty towards their biological parents. Your step-son probably views you as someone who is trying to replace his biological father. He may even see you as the cause for his parents' separation, even though this may not be true. Your presence in his mother's life may dash his hopes of seeing his parents reunite.

Give yourself time to build a relationship with him. He may view your attempt to control and discipline him as a threat. He may resent you for playing a father's role and may feel the need to 'fight you off'. View yourself as a mentor rather than as an authority figure. Initially, it may be best if you refrain from playing the disciplinarian role, as your step-son may not be able to accept you as an authority figure until you have earned his trust and respect.

Talk to him as often as you can on a one-to-one basis to build rapport. Some children may experience a loyalty conflict if they get along well with their step-parent. Emphasise to your step-son that you do not expect him to treat you as his real father. This is something you may have to reiterate several times.

Support his relationship with his biological father. When he puts you down or compares you to his father, try to understand his difficulties and not take it personally. Listen to him and empathise with his anger. Let him know hat you care about him although you are not his biological father. Over time, he will be able to read your good intentions and believe that you do love him. As a step-parent, you need to spend time with him doing positive daily activities so as to form a strong bond.

8.3   I HAVE ONE CHILD FROM MY PREVIOUS MARRIAGE AND MY BOYFRIEND HAS TWO. WE ARE GETTING MARRIED SOON BUT OUR CHILDREN DO NOT SEEM TO GET ALONG. I AM WORRIED ABOUT THEM. HOW CAN THIS NEW FAMILY WORK?

There are new relationships and dynamics to adjust to in a family of step-parents and step-siblings. As you and your partner come from two different households, you have to anticipate a wide range of differences in views, parenting styles and routines. Try to be patient and introduce changes slowly. Be prepared to weather a storm in the initial phases, when the children are all learning to adapt to a major change in their lives after having gone through the emotional strain of their respective parents' divorce.

For a start, step-parents need to smooth out some important issues to do with parenting, discipline and house rules. It is essential for them to iron out the differences so that there are standard rules and limits that each parent can enforce.

Bear in mind that there are circumstances in which step-siblings have to abide by different rules, according to their needs and ages. For example, a curfew for an 11-year-old child will be different from that for a 16-year-old teenager. Step-parents can conduct family meetings to brief the children on family rules, expectations and routines. State clearly what the consequences are if these rules are broken.

Many conflicts usually arise on the matter of disciplining the children. As a step-parent, you may sometimes give your step-children preferential treatment to avoid straining the relationship. However, this will cause your own children to resent you, or feel jealous and angry towards their step-siblings. Thus, having clear rules at home prevents you from favouring any child or being manipulated by any child.

It is important to note that the job of disciplining falls on the respective parent of each child and not on the step-parent. The parents should agree on the disciplinary limits of each step-parent. When the step-parent exercises that authority in the parent's absence, the parent should always back up his actions in front of the children, if that is in the child's best interest. This helps the children learn that they cannot play one parent against the other to get their way. Disagreements about discipline should be settled privately and not discussed in front of the children.

The key is to communicate with your new spouse. Do keep an open mind if your spouse raises a point about your child. Do not allow the children's discipline issue to become a source of tension in your marriage.

8.4 HOW CAN I HANDLE RIVALRY AMONG STEP-SIBLINGS?

Sibling rivalry is very common in families and even more so amongst step-siblings. Each child now has to deal with less living space and a greater need to share. They may quarrel over the use of the bathroom, computer or television. Ensure you take time to talk to them about how they feel being in this new family and how they view each family member. It is important to reinforce their role in the family and assure them that they will always be unique in your eyes.

Avoid pressurising step-siblings into accepting and liking one another. Engage in finding similar interests among them, so they will find it easier to break the ice and form closer bonds.

You could also consider:
- developing a new set of family traditions,
- planning something enjoyable for the whole family,
- letting the children take turns in deciding how to spend the weekend together.

In addition, each parent would do well to spend time alone with his or her step-children on a task or hobby. Try to see your step-children in a positive light and avoid making comparisons with your own children. Making a conscious effort to build rapport would help cultivate stronger family bonds for one another.

Guidelines for step-parents
- Introduce changes slowly.
- Establish clear rules.
- Support the children's relationship with their biological parent.
- Let children know that it is okay to talk about their non-custodial parent or about their new step-parent.
- Communicate individually with the step-children.
- Spend time together to cultivate common interests.
- Create new family traditions and do things together to build closeness.

HOW TEACHERS CAN HELP

As children spend almost a third of their day in school, teachers play an indispensable role in their lives. If you are facing problems with your child, consider getting in touch with either his form teacher or the school principal to discuss your concerns. Inform them of your marital situation and how you think your child may be affected. Explain to them the difficulties you are facing with your child and your worries.

9.1 WHAT ROLE CAN A TEACHER PLAY?

Teachers are quite experienced in picking up that something is wrong with a child. Some parents may find it hard to be frank with a teacher but they must bear in mind that some teachers go out of their way to ensure that children from broken homes get more attention and kindness.

The teacher can inform the parents if the child is experiencing behavioural changes or academic difficulties. If parents and teachers can intervene early, they can help the child adjust better to the divorce. On the teacher's part, he or she should keep the matter confidential. Children sometimes feel that there are few people they can turn to when they encounter problems. Besides parents, teachers are probably their next best option. Sometimes, a child may find it easier to talk to his teacher who can take on the roles of confidante and adviser.

9.2 HOW CAN A TEACHER ENGAGE THE CHILD?

Teachers can highlight a child's strengths and involve him in areas that he is good at so that he can develop self-esteem. Also, teachers can collaborate with parents to set limits on children who have become disruptive in class as a result of their parents' divorce.

Teachers can be more sensitive when discussing issues about families, especially if a child's parents had recently undergone divorce. Teachers can look out for emotional distress in children, or if they become easily distracted or irritable.

Nowadays, schools have trained and experienced counsellors to help children who are having emotional or behavioural problems. These counsellors can talk to the child and help him deal with the difficult issues in his life.

WHERE CAN I GO FOR SUPPORT?

PART 10

Some parents may feel that they need external help if they find that their child is not coping well with their divorce. When a child's behaviour becomes unmanageable, disruptive or even harmful, parents should consider seeing a professional counsellor.

10.1 HOW CAN PROFESSIONAL COUNSELLING HELP A CHILD WHOSE PARENTS ARE GOING THROUGH A DIVORCE?

Just as most people benefit from talking to someone when they run into problems or are worried about something, parents may get clearer answers or advice from a counsellor. Sometimes, talking through an issue enables parents to see things from a larger perspective. This may help them discover solutions to the problems that their child is facing. Sometimes, a problem may remain but the parent may leave the counsellor's office feeling emotionally stronger to deal with the issues at hand. It is important that parents get good counsel and it is sometimes better to seek professional help. A counsellor who is not emotionally entangled in a family's issues and who has a neutral perspective may help one to find balanced solutions to a problem.

10.2 HOW CAN A CHILD BENEFIT FROM SPEAKING TO A COUNSELLOR?

Children find it less threatening to talk to a trustworthy adult who is outside the family circle. This is especially the case when they are aware that their parents are in distress. They may not want to further upset their parents by unloading their worries on them.

Some children may be hesitant to discuss personal issues about their family, as they may feel guilty about 'betraying' the family and its secrets. In addition, a child whose parents are separated may be caught in a loyalty conflict between them. The child may not feel comfortable being honest with one parent about his feelings towards the other. In these circumstances, a professional counsellor may be the best option. The counsellor will be able to build rapport with the child and get him to disclose his feelings through a variety of play, art and verbal techniques.

10.3 HOW IS THE CHILD GUIDANCE CLINIC EQUIPPED TO HELP DISTRESSED CHILDREN?

The Child Guidance Clinic is the main specialist clinic in Singapore that assesses and treats emotional, behavioural and developmental disorders in children and adolescents up to the age of 18. Specialists at the clinic will look into the background of the child who is referred to them. They also listen to the parents' concerns before talking to the child on a one-to-one basis. The specialists may also have to help the child get over certain misconceptions. For example, some children mistakenly believe that when parents get a divorce, they will be sent to a children's home. The specialists will explain to the child what the usual living arrangements will be after his parents' divorce. This understanding often greatly reduces the child's anxiety and distress.

A child who blames himself for his parent's break-up is helped to understand that he is not responsible for it. This frees him from needless guilt and anxiety.

Specialists at the clinic also help parents understand what their child is going through. If necessary, parents are given individual counselling to deal with their loss and pain. An emotionally and physically strong parent is better able to take care of the child.

Parents often also bring their children to the clinic because of concerns about the divorce, custody or access privileges. Where possible, the specialist works with both parents and the children concerned to help them resolve the matter amicably. Such a positive approach is preferred, as it significantly reduces the children's distress over their parents' divorce. In cases, where the parents are caught in a bitter and acrimonious battle over custody or access matters, the court may request the psychiatrist to assess the situation and give his neutral opinion regarding the matter.

In Singapore and in many other countries, lawyers encourage their clients who are having conflicts regarding custody, access or maintenance matters to try mediation or a collaborative family approach to resolve their differences in an amicable way. The focus is on looking at the best interests of the child and resolving the relevant issues via negotiation, rather than through litigation.

HELP FOR PARENTS AND CHILDREN

Family Justice Courts Building
3 Havelock Square Singapore 059725. Tel: 6435 5110

PAVE (Family Violence Specialist Centre)
211 Ang Mo Kio Ave 3, #01-1446, Singapore 560211. Tel: 6555 0390

Help Every Lone Parent (HELP) Family Service Centre*
570 Ang Mo Kio Ave 3, #01-3317 Singapore 560570. Tel: 6457 5188

PPIS As-Salaam Family Support Centre*
322, Ubi Ave 1 #01-591 Singapore 400322. Tel: 6745 5862

Family Service Centres are neighbourhood-based social service agencies in Singapore that provide counselling and support for families in need of help. Those marked * provide services for single-parent families.

TELEPHONE HELPLINES

ComCare Call
Tel: 1800 222 0000

Tinkle Friend (for children aged 7 to 12 years)
Tel: 1800 2744 788 (free when calling from home line)
9.30 am – 11.30 am & 2.30 pm – 5.00 pm

TouchLine (for individuals aged 11 to 35 years)
Tel: 1800 377 2252
10.00 am – 10.00 pm

Samaritans of Singapore (24-hour crisis counselling centre)
Tel: 1800 221 4444

USEFUL RESOURCES

Books

Helping Your Kids Cope With Divorce The Sandcastles Way. M Gary Neuman & Patricia Romanowski. Random House (1998)

How To Help Your Child Overcome Your Divorce. Elissa P Benedek, MD & Catherine F Brown. American Psychiatric Press, Inc. (1995)

The Parents' Book About Divorce. Richard A Gardner, MD. Bantam Books (1991)

What To Tell The Kids About Your Divorce. Darlene Weyburne. New Harbinger Publications (1999)

Helping Mothers and Children Survive Divorce. Trish Mylan. Ministry of Community Development, Youth and Sports (2006)

When Parents Fight The Children Cry. Dr Cai Yiming. Hope Story (2005)

The Divorce Workbook For Children. Lisa M Scahb, LCSW. Instant Help Books (2008)

Websites

Family Justice Courts
www.familyjusticecourts.gov.sg
Provides information on legal procedures, and the help and programmes available.

AWARE (Association of Women and Research)
www.aware.org.sg/divorce/
Provides information on divorce and AWARE's services.

New York State Parent Education and Awareness Programme
www.nycourts.gov/IP/parent-ed/pdf/ParentsHandbook.pdf
Educates divorcing/separating parents about the impact of their break-up on their children.

Divorce Aid
www.divorceaid.co.uk/index.html
Provides information and resources on families undergoing divorce.

ABOUT THE AUTHORS

Dr Parvathy Pathy

Dr Parvathy Pathy is a child psychiatrist attached to the Child Guidance Clinic, Institute of Mental Health, Singapore. She received her basic and advanced medical degrees from the National University of Singapore and her postgraduate training in the area of child abuse and juvenile sex offending at the Royal Children's Hospital in Melbourne, Australia and the Young Abusers Project, London.

Dr Pathy counsels children, teenagers and their families who come to her with a wide range of emotional, psychological and behavioural problems. These include children who are struggling with their parents' divorce. Dr Parvathy Pathy also looks after abused children and conducts custody and access assessments for the Family Justice Courts, Singapore.

Dr Pathy has written two other books:
- *Kim's Story* (2002) – a short story about unconditional love and adoption
- *Living With Discipline Issues* (2015) – a book about effective discipline techniques for parents.

Dr Ann-Marie Lo Castro

Dr Ann-Marie Lo Castro has been a Principal Clinical Psychologist, Clinical Supervisor and Therapeutic Play Specialist at the Child Guidance Clinic since 2008. She holds a Master's Degree (cum laude) in Clinical Psychology Research; an MBA (cum laude) with research in Stress and Managed Health Care and in Social Science (clinical practice). Her PhD in Behavioural Medicine focuses on psychological variables in relation to breast cancer in women. She is also an Executive Business and Life Coach. She is passionate about people embracing change and reaching their maximum potential.

Dr Lo Castro is currently dedicated to therapeutic practice and intervention, to support children, with a range of psychological, behavioural and emotional issues. She also specialises in divorce and custody issues, complex trauma, and creative and expressive arts in therapy, to help children express their innermost feelings and thoughts. Motivated to explore answers to human behaviour, Dr Lo Castro follows scientific developments through NASA and has proposed a model for psychology and outer space to help with human resilience and coping behaviours. She attributes her achievements to the generous support of a loving family, her two beautiful children Marcello and Raffaella and the aesthetic value she attaches to life and the people around her.

Ms Foo Cirong

Ms Foo Cirong is a Medical Social Worker with the Child Guidance Clinic. As part of the youth forensic team, she provides support to parents or caregivers whose children may be struggling with abuse-related traumas or offending behaviours.

Ms Foo believes that positive relationships within families or communities are critical in   culties. In her work   d their children's   more effective co   aching families fro   on the resources